Praise for Jon Katz

"Jon Katz understands dogs as few others do, intuitively and unburdened by sentimentality. His keen insights cut to the heart of the human-pet relationship—its immense joys and painful sorrows. With wisdom and grace, he unlocks the canine soul and the complicated wonders that lie within and offers powerful insights to anyone who has ever struggled with, and loved, a troubled animal."
—JOHN GROGAN, author of *Marley & Me*

"Katz's world—of animals and humans and their combined generosity of spirit—is a place you're glad you've been."
—*The Boston Globe*

"One of our most talented and perceptive canine chroniclers."
—*AKC Gazette*

A Good Dog

A Good Dog

THE STORY OF ORSON,
WHO CHANGED MY LIFE

Jon Katz

RANDOM HOUSE TRADE PAPERBACKS
NEW YORK

2007 Random House Trade Paperback Edition

Copyright © 2006 by Jon Katz

All rights reserved.

Published in the United States by Random House Trade Paperbacks,
an imprint of The Random House Publishing Group,
a division of Random House, Inc., New York.

RANDOM HOUSE TRADE PAPERBACKS and colophon
are trademarks of Random House, Inc.

Originally published in hardcover in the United States by Villard Books,
an imprint of The Random House Publishing Group,
a division of Random House, Inc., in 2006.

ISBN 978-0-8129-7149-1

Printed in the United States of America

www.atrandom.com

2 4 6 8 9 7 5 3 1

Photographs by Peter Hanks

Book design by Susan Turner

To Brian McLendon,
for his unwavering faith in my work

LOVE MERCY

Do not be daunted by the enormity of the world's grief. Do justly, now. Love mercy, now. Walk humbly, now. You are not obligated to complete the work, but neither are you free to abandon it.

—TALMUD

AUTHOR'S NOTE

This is a memoir, a work of nonfiction. All the events I described happened; all the characters are real.

A few names have been changed. Carr, the farmer, didn't wish to be identified—due, he said, "to one or two outstanding debts." Everything he said or did, however, occurred as described.

The name of the holistic veterinarian in Vermont has been changed at her request, but her treatment of Orson is described as it occurred. I've also changed the names of the animal communicator, referred to here as Donna, and of the women who worked in the garden.

All the other names in the book are true to life, as is the story of Orson and me.

A Good Dog

Orson

A Dog Called Devon

My neighbor came pounding at the back door. "Devon is over at the school!" she shouted. "He's got a school bus trapped. They've called the police. You better get down there."

I didn't need to hear more. Ever since I'd brought him home, this new dog Devon was mesmerized by New Jersey's vast supply of things to herd and chase, things he'd never seen back in rural Texas: kids on skateboards and scooters, garbage trucks and snowplows, and buses.

He particularly loved buses.

Devon herded school buses at every opportunity. He could hear their throaty engines blocks away and began circling, offering the famed border collie eye. He had chased buses several times, once or twice halting them in the middle of the street.

By now, my wife and daughter and neighbors were used to seeing me tear after him through yards and across lawns, cursing and screaming, "Come!" and "Here!" and "Stop!"—any-thing I could think of to get his attention. Invariably, I failed.

Once I rushed out in horror to see him clamped onto a moving school-bus tire, hanging on while his body thumped onto the asphalt and then off. Fortunately, the bus was moving slowly. Devon was brave and determined, in his own way, and I was slowly grasping that my yard and its wooden picket fence were only mildly diverting amusements for him. He could burrow under the fence, nose its wooden slats apart, or, if all else failed, simply sail over it.

So I ran to the redbrick elementary school a couple of blocks from my home in Montclair, New Jersey. I could hear Devon barking as I got close.

A knot of anxious mothers had gathered there, agitated and upset. Montclair is not the kind of town that chuckles at the antics of demented border collies, especially when kids and school buses are involved. Devon was charging purpose-fully at the closed door, nipping as if the bus were a giant sheep, while the kids peered out the windows, shouting, and the driver held the door closed with his foot. Devon was a working dog with a purpose.

Outside, several mothers were circling their chicks, pok-ing and stomping at Devon, crying, "Get off!"

"This dog is dangerous!" I heard one woman yell. "Did you call the police?" The more the screaming intensified, the more excited and determined Devon seemed to become. He wasn't about to be run off by soccer moms or a bellowing bus driver.

I rushed up behind him, shouting, "It's okay, he's my dog, he won't hurt anybody." I even announced that he was a "rescue dog," usually a surefire way to win sympathy and support. But my reassurance didn't seem to ease the mothers' minds, and I can't say I blamed them. I knew Devon wouldn't hurt the kids, but how could they know?

I heard sirens in the not-too-distant distance. Could they really be coming for us? A red-faced teacher or administrator shouted, "Here come the police. Get back."

For somebody who had two mellow and responsive yellow Labradors, dogs whose greatest passions were eating and sleeping, this was high canine drama. I seemed to have suddenly acquired the John Dillinger of dogs.

The sirens sounded nearby as I rushed up behind Devon. I seized him by the collar and whacked him on the butt to get his attention. Startled, he looked at me, seeming to snap out of his trance. I'd neglected to grab a leash, so I picked him up, yelling silly platitudes to the angry parents and school officials.

"What the *hell* is wrong with you?" I hissed to this impossible dog. Then—I can't recall my thoughts, if I had any besides a vague fear that Devon would be marched off to the local animal shelter and imprisoned, perhaps even killed—I ran.

I took off, dog in arms, fleeing from the shouting kids, the ticked-off bus driver, and, especially, from the police. My only previous run-ins with the law had been traffic tickets; now I and my dog were fugitives.

Huffing and puffing—Devon probably weighed close to fifty pounds—I scuttled between the houses across from the school and then zigzagged like a burglar up driveways, down alleys, through lovingly tended backyards. Dogs barked, cats fled, a few people stuck their heads out their windows and stared.

One thing going for me was that New Jersey suburbs are densely built, with lots of gardens and garages to hide in. The people whose property I was invading wouldn't know we were on the lam; they probably just assumed I was crazy.

The sirens got closer. I prayed for a water-main break or a fender-bender, anything to distract the police; surely, they had more important things to do. But then the sirens stopped, suggesting the police had arrived at the school, and weren't rushing to some other crime scene.

This dog had been through a lot, and I wasn't going to let him go to jail. Sweating, my heart pounding, I kept moving, taking refuge in a garage a few blocks from my house.

I hoped my neighbors wouldn't turn me in—most had become fond of Devon . . . sort of. They'd learned that although eccentric, he wasn't dangerous. But I couldn't head home without drawing close to the school, risking apprehension by what I imagined was a burgeoning army of law enforcement and animal control officials. I could only guess how this was playing over police radios: *Crazed dog attacking children outside school.*

So I pushed Devon into a corner; holding him by the collar, I crouched down with him.

He licked my face frantically, a bit alarmed, I think, by my excited, fearful demeanor. Devon had a genius for getting into trouble, yet it also seemed to startle him that he had done wrong and upset me. The world appeared to make no sense to him.

"Don't move or I will beat you senseless, you crazy son of a bitch," I muttered. "You can't go herding school buses, you just can't. That was not a sheep!"

Looking at him, I was struck again by what a beautiful dog he was, black and white with a pronounced blaze on his chest. And by how much I had come to love him in so short a time. He had an elegant thin nose. His eyes were intense and beautiful, deep and black, and I saw a sweetness and sorrow in them, existing side by side with his craziness, which never failed to touch my heart. He seemed to expect to fail, a tough burden for a proud working dog. I wanted to help him succeed.

He had been with me just a few weeks, but we had grown attached, to say the least. When he wasn't chasing trucks or buses, he wanted only to be with me. His devotion was grounding, his affection comforting.

Huddled in our garage corner, he was all kisses, licking me, offering his belly for scratching. I took off my belt and looped it through his collar, fashioning a short leash.

After a moment's rest, we snuck out, crossed the street, and slunk into another garage. By now, Devon seemed to be getting the drill: skittering along beside me, stopping when I did, lying low.

Down the block, I glimpsed a police car, lights flashing, slowly cruising the quiet street. I didn't relish calling my wife to tell her Devon and I had been arrested for molesting a school bus. Thank God people in town rarely locked their garages. We were three blocks from the school, four or five from home.

We sat for more than an hour in the cool, dark space, Devon a perfect gentleman, sitting still, dozing a bit. He seemed to be enjoying our quality time. Already he could read me well. When I was upset with him—not a rare occurrence—he could be quite well behaved.

What an absurd position to be in, I thought. And yet it was a wake-up call of sorts, a jolt of reality. If I wanted to keep this dog, I was going to have to learn a lot more than I knew, do a lot better than I was doing.

My friend Nancy's house was just across the street. I peered both ways, saw no SWAT teams. Leading Devon by the belt, holding my pants up with one hand, I furtively rushed across the street and banged on her back door. Shocked, she took us in. Devon instantly took off after her cat, chasing her under the living room sofa.

When I collected him and told Nancy what had happened, she cracked up. It was, she said, the most ridiculous story she'd ever heard. "Go home," she said. "They aren't going to shoot you."

"This is serious," I insisted. "The police are looking for us. They'll take the dog. He stopped a school bus." Still incredulous but knowing how I already felt about this weird border collie, she grasped our plight. More than one neighbor would look the other way and help us out that spring.

A half-hour later, Devon and I were lying on the floor of Nancy's minivan, a blanket over the dog. She pulled up to my back door. Carrying the dog under the blanket, I scurried inside and put him in a crate in the basement. Then I let my two yellow Labs, Julius and Stanley—gentle as manatees—into the backyard. No school-bus marauders here, officer.

A few minutes later, a police car did swing by, and the cop paused to look at the Labs as they lumbered over to the gate, wagging. He smiled, waved, and I waved back. Then I visited Devon in the basement, alternately hugging and cursing him.

For several days afterward, Devon and I only walked around the neighborhood before dawn or after twilight, or drove to parks in other parts of town. We did not make the evening news, or even the weekly paper. The two of us didn't have much of a half-life as suburban desperadoes. Since no one was hurt, things died down. The police did, in fact, have better things to do.

But it was months before we walked past the school again.

I first heard of Devon when a border collie breeder in Texas e-mailed me. I had long been fascinated by the breed and I'd been corresponding with her for months about her dogs, but we had concluded—or so I thought—that border collies were not really a good fit for suburban New Jersey. We were right, too.

The breeder had read a book of mine in which I briefly described my life with Julius and Stanley. Like all good breeders, she had strong instincts about where her dogs ought to go. Now she was back in touch, saying she had a dog available, beautiful, bright, very dominant, a dog with . . . issues. She sensed we might be a match.

Devon was two years old and wicked smart, she said, and he needed a home. His life as an obedience show dog had crashed and burned. I still didn't know all the details, but he had somehow messed up and vanished from the obedience circuit. Now he needed badly to get out of town.

I was intrigued, even drawn to the idea, though clueless. I loved my Labs dearly, but they were undemanding and easily trained—in fact, they hadn't really required much training at all. They asked little of me beyond walks, treats, and companionship. They walked off-leash and never ran away, rarely barked, adored children, even those who pulled their tails or ears. They were delighted to encounter and greet joggers, landscape workers, and, especially, our neighborhood delivery people. The UPS and FedEx drivers kept a stash of biscuits for them. Sometimes—this was a secret—Julius and Stanley even rode with them in their trucks for a few blocks. The Labs would no sooner have halted a school bus than they would have jumped over the moon.

I couldn't explain to my wife, Paula—appropriately skeptical about the logic of bringing a troubled border collie into northern New Jersey—why I wanted this other dog.

I didn't know myself. It was just a feeling I had.

A few days later, Devon arrived at Newark Airport. In some circles, this part of the story is already well known.

Understanding little about this kind of dog, I opened the door of the transport crate to greet the just-unloaded Devon, and ended up on my butt, shocked, listening to the shrieks of travelers in vast Terminal C as this wolflike, black-and-white creature hopped from one baggage carousel to the next. Soon the Port Authority police were in pursuit. A portent, perhaps.

When Devon arrived, I was living restlessly in New Jersey, writing books and magazine articles and columns online, some about technology and what I felt was the great promise of the Internet and the World Wide Web.

My wife was a reporter working for *The Washington Post,* spending many of her days traveling in and out of New York City, about sixteen miles east of our town.

For years, my life had been structured around the care of our daughter—driving her to school and to the innumerable lessons, playdates, and activities that make up the lives of contemporary suburban children. Now she'd headed happily off to college and that role was gone. It left a big hole.

I was surrounded by people, but close to few. I had a couple of friends but, like so many men, little that was meaningful or honest to say to them. My troubled original family had died or drifted apart; the very notion of our family had disintegrated.

Like many people, we had gravitated to the suburbs to raise our kid, largely because we couldn't afford to live in New York City. Yet I felt out of sync there, an oddball in a place that seemed awfully straight. I didn't care about houses or lawns, and disliked the intensity of the obsession with children, even as I often succumbed to it.

I was well into midlife, learning how many clichés are true: Time was becoming a finite concept. I wasn't old yet, but neither did I have forever to do the things I wanted and still hoped to do. More than anything else, I didn't want to settle into a life of routine, passivity, and social and cultural ritual. I did not want to stagnate. I could envision spending my last years comfortably in New Jersey, harrumphing about change, walking the dogs four or five times a day, going to the movies on Friday, holing up in my basement trying to write—and I couldn't bear the thought.

I was becoming one of those people.

My life seemed to be slipping through my fingers while I doodled and dithered, and I began to believe that my father's hurtful, often-stated judgment of me from childhood was correct: I was not living up to my potential.

I actually had a recurring bad dream about collapsing from a heart attack on one of my innumerable walks through the neighborhood with the Labs.

I wanted—needed—my life to change, and it certainly did. The dog named Devon landed in the middle of my mundane, commonplace middle-class drama like a heat-seeking missile. I have had—and still have—many dogs, almost all of whom I loved dearly, but only one in my life so far was powerful enough to shake things up the way he did, to speak so directly, if unconsciously, to my heart.

Devon was instinctive and dominant, in the way of well-bred border collies—and explosive. As I learned that day at the school, you couldn't simply coexist with him, as you could with some dogs; you had to react to him. Like all border collies, he needed work. I didn't realize for some time that I was the work he would find.

Looking back on those first weeks together, I sometimes think he set out to take on, one by one, all the things that were troubling and challenging me—work, friends, drift and stasis—even though I have written and argued and believe that this can't really be so, that dogs can't think that way or set out to achieve such goals. Yet there's no denying what he wrought, even if I still can't quite comprehend it.

From the first, I loved that dog beyond words—an odd thing for a writer to say. He was a creature of my own unconscious in the way that some animals enter the deepest parts of lucky people's lives. Everything that happened after he entered my life was unexpected and surprising.

The dog named Devon came radiating crisis and mystery. Every time we surmounted one drama or persevered through joy or grief, I thought my life with him had at last entered a period of predictability and tranquility.

I was always wrong.

Orson, Rose, and Clem

CHAPTER ONE

A Dog Called Orson

Carolyn Wilki told the five of us to spread out into a circle in her pasture, with our dogs. We were an odd group, a motley mix of dog lovers and our anxious border collies and shepherds arrayed near an aging stone farmhouse in eastern Pennsylvania in the blazing summer sun.

The other four people did as instructed, along with their dogs. I didn't.

Devon and I were in our third month of working with Carolyn, a respected and fiercely opinionated sheepherder and dog behaviorist. She'd suggested that we join this herding class in addition to our weekly lessons. So we had, with trepidation. I'm not generally a joiner; I don't have a good history with groups. And Devon was not a dog who played well with others, either.

Once we were mostly in formation, Carolyn brought out

her antique metal box filled with small figures of dogs, sheep, and fences. I groaned.

Carolyn was fond of her toy farm creatures, which she'd shown me on our first visit, and loved to demonstrate the ballet that constituted sheepherding—human, dog, and sheep all moving in relation to one another. She would haul her box out and carefully place the components in their appropriate positions on a picnic table or on the grass. Then she'd sketch out herding and training moves like an NFL coach diagramming complex patterns for offense. The papers she handed her students when class ended were filled with X's and O's, squibbles and arrows. The X's were dogs, the O's were people. If the X's went here, she'd explain, then the O's would go there. The sheep were usually the squibbles.

Devon and I were rarely where we were supposed to be. He herded sheep the way he herded school buses—forcefully, impulsively, explosively. At least the sheep could run.

This role-playing was not the sort of thing either of us was especially good at. I was allergic to being lectured to, had hated just about every class and teacher I'd ever had, and the favor had been returned. Poor Mr. Hauser actually wept in front of my mother when I had to take his math class for the third time. Neither of us could bear the idea of going another round. Authority issues continued to plague me through my adult life. One reason that being a writer suited me was that most of the time the only jerk I had to put up with was me.

Devon had similar issues with commands and obedience. Training seemed to either upset or excite him, and learning to herd sheep seemed unlikely to be an exception.

"You are a ewe," Carolyn told me, pointing to an O on her diagram, and placing one of her tiny white plastic sheep along a toy fence. "You will stand over here and wait to be approached by a dog," she said, gesturing to an eighty-year-old woman in a sun hat holding a terrified sheltie on a leash.

Everybody else seemed willing, even enthusiastic, about acting out these herding moves. But I didn't want to be a ewe. Devon looked up at me curiously; I knew there was no way he was going to do this, either.

In fact, he suddenly charged after the sheltie, chasing him under Carolyn's truck. I pulled him back, made him lie down, and he settled to watch the proceedings.

As Carolyn passed by, dispensing instructions, I whispered—hoping to avoid a scene—that I didn't want to be a ewe, or to play this game. Carolyn did not suffer fools or rebels gladly. "I don't care what you want," she muttered. "Do it. It will be good for you."

I couldn't. No better at being submissive than this strange dog I now owned, I told Carolyn this wasn't the right class for me. Devon and I retreated to our room (Carolyn's Raspberry Ridge Farm is a bed-and-breakfast as well as a training center) to brood. I put Devon in his crate and lay down on the bed. Outside the window, I could hear the "dogs" and "sheep" going through their exercises as Carolyn offered suggestions and critiqued the proceedings. Much as I often wished for a more pliant dog, I also wished I were a more compliant human. Life would be smoother.

It's an article of faith among trainers that the problem with dogs is almost always the people who own them. My dog and I were both impulsive, impatient, distractible, and restless. That was why we'd come.

Carolyn was an impassioned believer in positive rewarding training, a training method that emphasizes reinforcing appropriate and desired behaviors, and generally rejects negative or coercive methods like yelling, swatting, or even more abusive responses.

Positive reinforcement puts pressure on the human, rather than the dog, to suppress anger and impatience, and simply praise or mark good behaviors—with words of praise, food, clickers, whatever works. It asks a lot of people; they have to take a long view of training and curb some of their stronger instincts. For somebody who is by no means an all-positive person, like me, it was difficult—especially with a dog like Devon, who daily challenged one's patience.

One afternoon he escaped the yard in New Jersey (I have no idea how), and soon afterward I heard the by-now-familiar screaming and tumult in the street and went running out. Devon had intercepted half a dozen Jersey teenagers on skateboards, rounded them up into a tight cluster in the center of the street—skateboards flying in every direction—and held everyone there until I arrived.

Carolyn would not have approved of my response, which was not positive in the least. I screamed at Devon to get away from the kids, apologized profusely, and retreated into the house, Devon in tow. The kids thought it was funny; when they got home, their parents might not.

Recognizing that I needed help with Devon, a far greater challenge than my mellow Labradors, I'd started bringing him to Raspberry Ridge, along with my younger border collie, Homer. Homer didn't seem destined to be an ace herder, either, but he was much more attentive and controllable than Devon.

Carolyn often said she was surprised that I'd stuck it out with Devon's lessons; in fact, she told me, she'd doubted I would come back after the first session. Which had been marked by Devon's chasing her panicked sheep around a fenced pasture. The truth is, I never thought of leaving Raspberry Ridge. Eventually, we became regulars.

From the first time we drove down the long gravel driveway, I was drawn to the place. Carolyn had an old stone farmhouse, a giant barn and other teetering outbuildings, a junkyard, perhaps two hundred ewes and rams, an old donkey, a dozen or so dogs, and more than seventy acres of grass, meadow, and woods.

She lived upstairs in the farmhouse; guests and visitors occupied the B&B rooms downstairs. She kept crates tucked all over the house, in which her herding dogs—border collies and shepherds—slept while waiting to work, exercise, or play.

These working dogs, I'd come to learn, led lives very different from my dogs'. Carolyn let them out several times a day to exercise and eliminate, but generally, they were out of crates only to train or herd sheep. While they were out, Carolyn tossed a cup of kibble into their crates for them to eat when they returned. I asked her once if she left lights on for the dogs when she went out, and she looked at me curiously. "Why? They don't read."

They were happy dogs nonetheless, fit and obedient, sociable with dogs and people. From Carolyn's example, I was learning to respect the true nature of dogs: they are wonderful, but they're still animals, and not even the most complex animals. She didn't see them as four-legged versions of humans, and woe to the student who did.

Still, they were everywhere. If you bumped into a sofa it might growl or thump. Some of her crew were puppies; some were strange rescue dogs.

The chief working dog was Dave, a venerable shorthaired Scottish border collie who efficiently ran the farm, moving sheep in and out of pastures and into training pens for lessons and herding work. This was an impressive fellow. I once saw a near-riot break out during a herding trial when some sheep crashed through a fence by the parking area, which was crammed with dogs, handlers, spectators, cars and trailers, and food stands. Carolyn yelled to me to run inside—Dave's crate held the place of honor by Carolyn's desk—and let him out.

When I opened the crate, Dave promptly rushed to the front door, pushed open the screen, and picked his way among the rampaging dogs and sheep and people. He gathered up the sheep and, at Carolyn's direction, moved them down the drive and into the back pasture, maneuvering them around lawn chairs and tents, barking dogs, and all the paraphernalia of a trial. He held them there until Carolyn arrived to close the pasture gate. Then he trotted right back to the house, nosed open the screen door, and went back into his crate. Dave was the anti-Devon, as grounded as Devon was excitable, as obedient as Devon was unresponsive, as useful as Devon was difficult and unpredictable. I told myself he was less interesting, too.

Carolyn's hallways were hung with crooks, ropes and halters, flashlights and rain gear. She loved dogs the way great trainers do, respecting their animal natures, understanding their simple and sometimes crass motives, accepting them as they are, rather than trying to recast them into versions of ourselves. The signs of her success with this approach were also abundant: the walls were festooned with trial ribbons and awards.

Yet she spent much of her time working with less heralded dogs and their desperate people. Troubled dogs from all over the country came riding up her driveway. I remember one pair of newlyweds who arrived with a schnauzer that had belonged to the bride. The groom was covered in bandages. It seemed that every time he tried to touch his wife, the dog bit him.

Why, someone asked, didn't they get rid of the dog? The bride was incredulous. "I love my husband, but this dog has been with me for years."

Carolyn prescribed an elaborate new regimen in which all food came from the husband's hand, and only when the dog was calm and well behaved. Any growling or biting meant the dog didn't eat. The couple stayed at Raspberry Ridge for a week, and when they drove away, the dog was dozing lovingly in the husband's lap, marriage saved.

Often, I was appointed "dog bait" for a weekend: I approached an aggressive dog with a bag of meatballs to see how close I could get before the dog went off. Meatballs and other smelly stuff were a centerpiece of Raspberry Ridge dog training. When an aggressive dog was on hand, all of us armed ourselves with meatballs and began approaching the dog from a distance, tossing meatballs, getting a bit closer each time. The dog would begin by barking, but as meatballs began to rain from the sky, he'd calm down and likely rethink his hostility to people.

Staying at Carolyn's bed-and-breakfast with Devon and Homer was an adventure. Sometimes, when I took the dogs out, I would hear Carolyn or somebody scream "Run!" and realize an aggressive dog-in-rehab was outside. We'd dive back inside, slamming the door as some ferocious-sounding creature thudded against it. These were exotic experiences for me, but useful for Devon, who became more comfortable on a farm and seemed rattled by fewer things.

The true heart of Carolyn's farm was her kitchen, where sausages and pungent dog treats lay scattered over the counters, along with collars, magazines and books, trial application forms, checks from her students (Carolyn, not big on details, often left them lying around for months), leashes, and dog toys.

Pots of coffee were always brewing, and dog people could be found sitting around her big wooden table at all hours. Devon and I were always welcome there, and he grew to love going around the table from person to person, collecting pats and treats. Troubled dogs were familiar at that table, and appreciated. If we couldn't bring our dogs many places, we could always bring them here. If Devon wasn't always successful, he was always accepted.

So was I. Here, I could be me. I came to cherish more rural pleasures. I began staying at the farm overnight, combining our lessons with taking the sheep out to graze. I helped with lambing in the spring, tossed hay to the flock in the winter. I met and befriended a donkey named Carol.

I also started accompanying Carolyn to the Scottish "faires" held around the region on weekends. She got paid peanuts for these appearances, but she loved showing people the art of herding, keeping it alive.

We would pile several dogs and half a dozen sheep into her pickup, along with hay and water and some temporary fencing, and drive off to herding demos. Suburbanites loved to see Dave push the sheep around parks and fields; between acts, Carolyn and I, like old-fashioned carnies on the circuit, could lounge in lawn chairs BS-ing about dogs.

While faires were child's play for Dave, the awed crowds responded as if they were at the Olympics. I understood: there is something profoundly beautiful and moving in seeing dogs do this traditional work. Devon could not herd in these situations—too dangerous—but he very much appreciated coming along, and was much hugged and admired. Even within the safer confines of Raspberry Ridge, his herding progress was uneven, to say the least. We had many frustrating and uncomfortable days, along with our triumphant moments.

Devon still wasn't reliable enough to herd the sheep, but if I put him on a leash, the sheep would move ahead of us anyway. We could take them out to pasture, then take up positions between the herd and the road.

It was often freezing, or sticky-hot and buggy, but if we went very early in the morning when the pasture was often shrouded in dew and mist, we could sit side by side for hours, Devon as calm as I ever saw him, listening to the sheep crunch away at the grass.

But when it was time to herd back to the barn and I released him, he would bore straight into the middle of the flock, all training forgotten, scattering sheep in every direction.

Homer was more of a herding dog, calmer, able to slip in behind the sheep and move them. He had more protective instincts, too; he could locate a newborn lamb off in the woods, help gather the flock in the midst of a blizzard.

But he also had problems. Homer was small, not especially hardy for a border collie, so he had trouble getting out in front of the sheep to turn the herd. He tended to use his mouth instead, and when he got excited, he'd grip a sheep by the legs—a major transgression. And he was easily intimidated. It was his misfortune to grow up as the Helldog's little brother. Devon relentlessly terrorized poor Homer, grabbing his toys and food, pinning him to the ground when he came near me. If his canine sibling could push him around, a cranky ram or ewe could intimidate him, too.

I knew neither dog would make a stellar working dog like Dave—they were already too old, too far down the path of pet-hood. And I didn't know enough to train them well. If I ever got serious about sheepherding, I would have to get a dog from a herding line and learn much more.

But we kept at it. At Raspberry Ridge, we saw an astonishing parade of dogs who bit, chewed, barked, and otherwise challenged the limits of their owners' love and responsibility. Carolyn took on one problem dog after another, stalking the farm in an Australian slouch hat and cape, pockets stuffed with smelly meat, analyzing behavior both canine and human, offering suggestions and instructions. Dogs paid attention to her. She understood them and their foibles, even as she often got frustrated with their humans.

Carolyn believed that in Devon's case "the world makes no sense to him." I thought she was correct. Devon faced a constant tension between being himself and trying to be what the world wanted him to be. He was always struggling to figure things out, always making choices, usually the wrong ones. I felt that herding sheep might help steady him.

Carolyn kept our lessons brief and focused. We usually took Devon into a pen with a few sheep and tried to induce him to move calmly around them. Usually we failed.

We supplemented that with grounding and obedience exercises—lie down, stay, get back. Eye contact. Name recognition. Over and over. It got boring, frustrating. I wasn't really prepared for how repetitive the proper training of a dog is, how long it takes, especially with an already-damaged student. I wanted training to be quick and painless.

Instead, it was difficult and challenging. Devon's sheep-herding skills improved only sporadically, and I could hardly call him obedient. But he loved working with me, and he did begin to calm down. I believed, though our progress was slow, that there was hope, that I was learning enough about dogs to train him and, therefore, to keep him.

I knew that my problems were as entrenched as his. I got angry and frustrated and yelled at Devon. Carolyn repeatedly pointed out that he wouldn't settle down until I did, but that was a tough lesson to translate into word and deed. Dogs like Devon, I've come to understand, feed off our attention to them. The more apoplectic I became when he didn't behave, the more I reinforced his misbehavior. Yet sometimes I found it impossible to remain quiet.

Once, out in the pasture, he tore off after a ewe, grabbed her leg, and tried to pull her down. Even from some distance away, I could see that he'd drawn blood, and I was horrified, enraged. I tore off after him, grabbed him by the collar, and screamed "No!" "Bad!" and the other useless things frustrated humans shout at their dogs. I knew by then that the right thing to do was to ignore the charging and biting, to wait for Devon to be calm around the sheep, then praise him. But I'm not sure I'll ever be able to summon such self-control at a moment like that.

Devon froze, frightened and cowering, as the ewe ran off. When I saw the look on his face, I stopped yelling and pulled him toward me, as upset with myself as I was with him. I knew this outburst would undermine our work together. I knew he couldn't help himself. I hated seeing the sheep bleed and limp, but I also hated screaming at him; I hated the rage and frustration I felt. Was this why we were coming out here? So I could bully him into submission?

I rocked Devon in my arms like a baby while he licked my face. "I will try to never do this again," I said. "I will try to be different."

I told Carolyn what had happened, and in her usual blunt way, she told me I had set things back months. "But it happens. You are, unfortunately, a human," she said. People, she pointed out, simply don't grasp that dogs faced with anger and menace have only two options: fight or flight. When you pummel or intimidate them, they might do one or the other, but they do not learn.

Still, it was there, at Carolyn's place, that I really got hooked on doing this ancient work with dogs, however haltingly we were learning it. And there I learned to love the rituals and routines of a farm. But it was also at Raspberry Ridge that I entered—or perhaps descended into—the world of dog lovers.

We would sit around her kitchen table for hours—Carolyn, her friends and students, the ceaseless parade of dog people who came to the farm—gabbing about our dogs, our training, what worked and what didn't. Almost everybody had a Devon-type dog, an animal they loved dearly but were struggling to live with.

We were outwardly different—rural and urban, men and women, old and young, doctors and farmers. We never talked about politics, work, or the outside world. Few of us brought spouses or kids along. These were dramas that involved just us and our dogs. We shared horror stories and triumphs; we argued incessantly about food and vets, leashes, litters and training. What worked? What had we learned that might be useful to others? How far were we prepared to go?

One morning at breakfast, I surprised myself by suddenly asking: "How many of you come from troubled families?" Every hand went up. We didn't pursue the topic, yet it was occurring to me—along with the other things I was starting to understand out there—that the emotional geography between people and their dogs was complicated and intriguing.

Faith and commitment kept us all coming back to Carolyn's fields—sometimes wiltingly hot, sometimes icy and bitter—to work hour after hour, week after week, with our dogs. Some of them would come running happily when their owners called. (Mine wouldn't.) Some would skillfully and instinctively herd sheep. (Not mine.)

But none of us were inclined to give up on our dogs. If anything, my love for Devon deepened as we struggled to work together and figure each other out. We attended weekly sessions, weekend sessions, and special weeklong training camps. We took the sheep out again and again.

I never managed to learn long division, but I couldn't soak up enough dog stuff. From the first, Carolyn had challenged my notion of Devon as a rebellious adolescent, pointing out how stressed, confused, and aroused he was by all my bumbling gesticulation, yelling, and ignorance. I'd come to understand that training him was less about his obedience than about my ability to become a better human, less angry and demanding, more patient and clear.

I saw that there were many successes, but also lots of failures. In some cases, Carolyn could find a simple key to turning a dog around. Many dogs left the farm in a few days, their problems markedly eased.

But sometimes it took years. Sometimes it never happened. People ran out of money, time, or emotional energy.

Dogs disappeared, or were given away, or, in extreme cases, put down. Still, how hard we worked. We were generous, praising others' dogs, cheering one another on, rooting for dogs and people to make it. Devon and I had joined a tribe.

The training began to take up a good chunk of my life, Devon and Homer and I whizzing back and forth along I-80. It took more than an hour just to reach the farm from our house, and training sessions took the better part of an afternoon or evening.

I had one measurable goal: that Devon win at least one herding ribbon before we were done. I didn't really care about the trophy, but passing a beginner's trial was something of a benchmark, a test of what I could learn and teach, of how much I could change. And I wanted Devon to be—and feel like—a winner, just once. Then, in my canine fantasy, we would retire to the normal life of a human and his beloved pet.

Away from Raspberry Ridge, my months with Devon remained tumultuous. He broke through a leaded-glass window when a UPS man came onto the front porch. He took off after dogs, cats, and wildlife. He somehow learned to open the door of our refrigerator, lifting containers of chicken and turkey burgers, neatly consuming the contents, and hiding the packaging strategically around the house, under the sofa or behind a chair.

One morning, out doing errands, I bought a sandwich for Paula at the neighborhood deli. Devon came along for the ride, as usual. After picking up the sandwich and stashing it in the car, I made stops at the hardware store and post office.

Back at the house, I discovered the sandwich was intact—except for the ham, which had vanished.

Our walks were dramas. For years, my Labs and I had ambled through the neighborhood, Julius and Stanley pausing to greet their many admirers and sniff the occasional bush, while I used our strolls to think about my writing. The dogs required little vigilance.

Devon, however, would wait until I wasn't paying attention, then pop the leash from my hand and tear into backyards to snatch food from barbecue grills, herd terrified lap dogs, or run down squirrels.

Gradually, our house became a minimum-security canine facility. Child locks appeared on the refrigerator and cupboard doors, Plexiglas panels over the leaded glass, bungee cords across the closets. Peace finally came, to a degree, when I bought some dog crates and put Devon inside one whenever I left the house.

It was hard to stay angry, anyway. He was extraordinarily loving. In the car, he loved to ride with his head on my shoulder, as if navigating. While I worked, he curled up at my feet.

He was always watching and studying me, aware of my every move, insistent on being only inches away. Yet our many moments of attachment and affection were punctuated by recurring outbursts of demonic behavior.

His first year with me provided nearly a lifetime of dog experiences. My Labs, Julius and Stanley, both died, Stanley of heart disease, Jules of cancer. Homer was my attempt to fill that void. But by year's end, I was starting to wonder whether I could live a peaceful, happy existence with Devon.

My first attempt to win Devon a herding-trial ribbon did

not go well. Stirred up even more than usual by the crowd, the other dogs, the competitive tension, he managed to knock over the judge. The panicked sheep busted through the corral gate and ran for their lives. "Thank you," said the judge—code for "Get lost, you are disqualified." I was also reprimanded for giving improper commands, like "*Get* those fucking sheep"—considered unsuitable for family sporting events. We regrouped and decided, despite our mortifying debut, to try again at the next trial, six months later.

It was during one of our innumerable and largely unsuccessful efforts to get Devon to lie down around sheep and stay calm that Carolyn noticed something: Whenever I gave Devon a command by name, he reacted by wincing, panting, cringing, or blinking—all signs of canine stress.

Devon didn't take to training sessions, even when undertaken with food or with that chirpy voice many trainers recommend and I hate. Some obedience-trained dogs, Carolyn said, associate training with unpleasantness, and Devon looked like one of them. Training made him anxious, as if he expected something bad to happen to him.

What about changing his name? "Let's start over," she suggested. "Then you can train him in a more positive way, without any baggage."

It seemed a strange idea. Change my dog's name? Wouldn't that just confuse him?

"Not at all," Carolyn said, pointing out that millions of rescue dogs were happily re-homed and renamed every year.

I didn't really see Devon as an "abused" or rescued dog. I thought the term overused, I told her, often an excuse for people who didn't train their dogs, preferring to regard them instead as piteous, helpless creatures.

Devon wasn't piteous, I argued. He was ferociously independent, athletic, bright, and intense. Though he'd had his share of trouble, I didn't want to think of him (or myself) as crippled or pathetic.

"Look, he shows every sign of stress when you talk to him," Carolyn replied. "Most of that is probably what happened to him before you got him. Some of it you and your big mouth and your impatience and anger. It all comes through to him; he's not a stupid dog. Let's begin again."

In fact, she was so high on the idea, she suggested it to the owners of a sheltie, shepherd, Bouvier, and border collie who were also at the farm for training that weekend. They all instantly shook their heads; it just struck them as extreme. But Carolyn was nothing if not an outside-the-box thinker, a quality I respected.

Why *not* change his name? Devon had always sounded a bit Martha Stewarty to me, anyway.

What should I call him instead? I've always admired Orson Welles, partly because he seemed another example of sadly unfulfilled potential.

"Okay," I said. "Let's go for it. How long will it take?"

Not long, Carolyn said, smiling, reaching for her meatball pouch. Devon knew exactly what this pouch was and always focused when her hand neared it. I'd gotten one like it, attached to my belt, usually stuffed with liver treats. Devon was staying much closer to me on walks these days.

Carolyn and I took out our pouches on a breezy, beautiful spring day, and as the wind ruffled the meadow and her sheep grazed peacefully, we took turns standing over this intensely focused and suddenly quite happy dog, taking turns saying *Orson,* and popping a meatball or a liver treat into his waiting mouth.

We only had to empty her pouch and mine once to make

the switch. Within twenty minutes, his name was Orson. He answered to it, made eye contact when I said it, and more significantly, associated it with nothing but good stuff.

If I kept my voice normal and cheerful when I said his name, there was no wincing, flattened ears, or averted eyes. Suddenly, training was about meatballs and liver treats, not about anger, disappointment, stress, or failure.

I can't claim he became a well-behaved dog in that pasture, but he began to be a different one. He looked at me more readily when I spoke his name, came when I called him, walked more closely by my side. Training began to be something he seemed pleased about and wanted to do, rather than something that made him cower and skulk.

His name became a good thing, something likely to bring reward and praise, not punishment and recrimination. It was an opportunity for me, too, to make good on my promise to do better by him.

So he became a dog called Orson.

In the fall, I entered Orson in a beginner's herding trial conducted under American Kennel Club auspices at Raspberry Ridge. The judges flew in from all over the country, and entrants and their dogs assembled from everywhere.

The beginner's protocol was fairly simple. You and your leashed dog entered a small fenced ring—perhaps seventy-five feet long and twenty-five feet wide—with traffic-type cones at either end. Unleashed, the dog had to lie down and then, at your command, go behind the five sheep in the pen and move them to the other end. After you and the dog had steered the sheep the length of the ring and around the cones three times, the dog had to lie down and stay; then you leashed him up and left the pen.

The trick was to get the dog to lie down and stay while you headed for the first cone. The dog had to be still, but the human had to keep moving, since dog and sheep had no idea where to go otherwise and couldn't get into a natural rhythm.

Beginner's trials were looser, less formal than other trial levels. Judges, if they were in a good mood, would cut you some slack. Or so I hoped.

Sheep can read dogs quite well, and when they see crazy ones, they move quickly. This was one of the big problems in working with Orson—the minute you walked through a gate, the sheep took one look and started running. That got him excited, and moving too quickly. Then I would start yelling, and things would deteriorate from there.

Still, I'd mailed in applications for both my border collies. Homer, less antsy, had a reasonable shot at fulfilling his herding destiny, at least at this introductory level. Orson was always a question mark, but I thought we'd take another shot. A ribbon—if we earned one—would be emblematic of my love for him, a recognition of the hard work Carolyn and I and Orson had been doing.

Even with a grounded dog, herding sheep is a tough thing to do. With a dog like Orson, it would be a milestone for both of us.

Homer, scheduled for the first trial day, had, true to form, acquitted himself fairly well. We'd gone through our paces quietly. I had trouble getting him to lie down, and he'd missed one of the cones on the third pass, but he was unaggressive and eager to please. I swear he actually seemed proud when he got his green-and-white ribbon that meant he was a qualified, though novice, herding dog.

But I was nervous on the second morning, when Orson's trial was scheduled. About a hundred people and thirty or forty dogs had gathered around the ring.

Orson normally would have gotten distracted and overexcited being around so many people and dogs, but he was relatively calm. In a funny way, he really did seem reinvented, or perhaps reincarnated, after his name change. He was less tense. My communications with him had changed, too, and were less fraught. Since "Orson" was free of unhappy associations, he paid more attention to me, responded more quickly, and seemed to even enjoy our training sessions and the rain of treats that often accompanied them. It wasn't so much that he had become a different dog but that the dog Orson really was had begun to emerge. I had more confidence that he would listen; he had more confidence that he could succeed.

But this would be a trickier and much more public test, with no treats allowed. We entered the gate, Orson on a leather lead, my number, 261, affixed to my shoulder with an elastic band. The judge nodded, and took a good look at Orson. "Pretty dog," he said.

"Lie down," I said, quietly, to Orson. He did. Then he stood up. Then he lay down. We went through this two or three times, until I lightly flicked his butt with my fingertips and said, "Hey! Lie down!" The judge smiled. Unlike Homer, Orson didn't seem at ease in the ring, but at least he wasn't out of control. So far, reasonably good. Then I told him to stay, went out to the sheep, and, since my voice often aroused him, used a hand command to tell him to come toward me. He took off like a rocket and headed for the sheep. Remembering Carolyn's injunction to keep moving, I scrambled from one orange cone down to the other, hooves and paws clopping behind me. The sheep whizzed past, followed by Orson-on-the-run.

"Yo," I yelled, and he turned and stopped. "Down." To my surprise, he dropped. Then I ran to the opposite cone, turned, said, "Okay, you're free," and dashed back toward the first cone, then around again. The sheep were shuttling along, though I thought I saw Orson bearing in on one of them.

"Orson," I said, holding up my hand. "Stay!" He looked at me, then at the sheep, then at me—and he stayed. I came around, slipped the lead back on him, and headed for the gate.

It was not an elegant performance—the judge was struggling to keep from laughing—but it seemed to me that we had done it: had lain down, stayed, moved the sheep three times, lain down, stayed, left. And nobody, human or animal, had gotten injured. Still, it was hardly textbook herding. I wasn't sure it qualified as herding at all. I had seen judges fail more-polished dogs for lesser infractions.

This judge said nothing, so I didn't know until after all the entrants had finished how we'd fared.

When the results were announced, the judge said "261" and handed me another green-and-white ribbon. Orson, too, had passed the beginner's test. He was a herder, sort of. I gave him a big hug, and he gave me a sloppy slurp. He seemed happy to get away from the trial ring.

Carolyn came running up, gave me a squeeze and critiqued my performance. I'd moved the wrong way and too slowly, she said, but not bad. On to the intermediate trials, she said.

I told her, thankfully, that this was the first thing I'd ever won. It was definitely my first victory together with Orson, who was enjoying pats and praise from the spectators. Yet I, too, was happy to get away.

Afterward, I put Orson on a long leash and we took Carolyn's sheep out for some grazing. We climbed the rise overlooking the far pasture, and the sheep spread out to eat. From my backpack I took a plastic bowl and some bottled water. I poured him some and drank some myself, then gave him a biscuit while I ate a cookie.

Orson sighed, and stretched out next to me, his head resting on my thigh. He paid no attention to the sheep, who crunched steadily ahead of us. He was soon asleep, and at peace.

I didn't see as much of Carolyn or Raspberry Ridge after that trial weekend. Carolyn saw herding trials as important yardsticks of training progress, especially for working dogs, but I didn't like trialing, and I don't think Orson did, either. He tensed up when he saw gates and fences and crowds of anxious people with dogs by their sides. Name change or not, he knew potential trouble when he saw it.

Besides, trials can sometimes inject an unappealing element into the relationship between human and dog. People like me tend not to simply enjoy the experience; we want to win. When we lose—sure to happen eventually—how can our disappointment and frustration not be apparent, especially to dogs, who read us skillfully?

I liked Carolyn's ideas about positive-reinforcement training, yet I was growing increasingly resistant to particular philosophies for training dogs. No single idea seemed appropriate for Orson and me. My own frailties kept me from being positive and patient enough, for example. Yet I was curious about the process. I was coming to have my own training approaches and wanted to explore them on my own.

Besides, I'd been bitten by another bug, once I realized how much I loved working on Carolyn's farm. I owned a tiny cabin in upstate New York and was hearing a great deal about the dairy farmers going under all around. Real estate in Washington County was still remarkably affordable. Why not pursue my ideas up there, on my own farm, with my own sheep, battered truck, fences, barns, and dogs?

I came up with several reasons why I should get my own small farm. Our cabin was too small for Paula to work in, with little space for my daughter or her friends. The property, with just two steeply sloping acres, was too small for sheep, too. And the cabin was geographically so cut off from the nearby town that I hardly knew anyone around me. I hadn't found lasting community in New Jersey or most of the other places we'd lived, but I still hoped for it. Perhaps up there.

Besides, on our own farm Orson could learn to herd, could have all the space even a demented border collie could want, could be far from school buses and sirens. He would, at last, learn to make sense of the world.

Winston

CHAPTER TWO

Orson and Winston

A little over two years after Orson arrived at Newark Airport, he and I were standing by a sprawling old farmhouse in the tiny hamlet of West Hebron, New York. This time I'd really done it. I'd bought a farm.

I will be a long time sorting through the process that led from there to here, but it went something like this: Orson's arrival in my life challenged me in any number of ways. To keep him, to do right by him, I began sheepherding with Carolyn Wilki.

Working with her, I became fascinated by the spiritual nature of training a dog. Two species trying to communicate with each other—it was a strange but powerful and alluring challenge. I also came to love the rhythms and satisfactions of farm life.

Before long, I began writing about dogs. I met and befriended scholars, breeders, behaviorists, vets, and dog lovers by the thousands, in person and online.

A researcher bombarded me with studies, surveys, and academic journal articles on dog behavior, genetics, and the human-animal bond. I was invited to training and veterinary conferences.

My own dog life had changed radically, continuously. After Julius and Stanley, the two Labs who'd lived so amiably with me when Orson arrived, had died, Homer had entered the household, but he was still struggling to coexist with so dominant a brother as Orson. Now, just before we decamped to the farm, another border collie, named Rose, had joined us—a configuration that, in the way of life with dogs, did not last long.

I'd named this place in honor of West Hebron's main intersection, known as Bedlam Corners, home to its only retail establishment, the Bedlam Corners Variety Store. Bedlam Farm.

A century ago, Hebron was so busy it was hard to cross the road; the intersection deserved its moniker. (The word *bedlam* evolved from the name of the world's first insane asylum in seventeenth-century London.) Now you could sit on a lawn chair for a half hour and not see much activity at that intersection, but Bedlam seemed a particularly apt name for Orson and me.

Three months earlier, we'd left the cabin I owned in nearby Cambridge, New York, where I'd written several books, and set out, drawn by mysterious impulses and instincts, to explore Hebron, an out-of-the-way, economically struggling mill town near the Vermont border.

"Hebron?" my neighbor in Cambridge had sniffed. "That's *really* the sticks. Nobody goes out there."

Hebron was, in fact, on the way to nowhere, but was reportedly beautiful, a sort of fading Brigadoon. As the locals put it, it was as country as dirt.

As we drove down Route 30, Orson rode in his customary position, sitting in the backseat of the truck, his head on my right shoulder, navigating. We passed a faded sign on the edge of the village: HEBRON 1786. Unless you were looking for Hebron, you had no real reason to visit or travel through it. But if you did, you couldn't help being drawn to it.

Like almost all agricultural areas upstate, Hebron was poor. Family farming was dying out, and no industry had replaced it. People undertook long commutes to Vermont or Saratoga Springs for work. The young pulled up stakes altogether. New York City weekenders were beginning to show up and make retreats out of bankrupt dairy farms, but they were few.

I gazed around at the stately old farmhouses, soft green pastures bounded by rolling hills, ponds, and lakes—and felt I'd somehow come home.

I noticed cows tied up in some backyards, chickens crisscrossing the road, a dog strolling down the middle of Route 30. The town clerk, it appeared, was also the town barber and beautician. Farmhouses with acreage still cost less than a two-car garage in New Jersey.

I could see the town's sadder attributes, too, the grinding poverty of trailers and cabins nestled in the woods without plumbing. Winters, I already knew, were brutal here, the winds screeching through these valleys, the hilly roads steep and slick. Stopping at the Variety Store for a soda, I heard that a huge bear had been spotted out on Chamberlin Mills Road.

I called a real estate agent on my cell phone.

I understood viscerally that this trip was more than a

house-hunting expedition. It was one of those fliers you take if you are fortunate, crazy, and determined not to do what's expected, which is to settle into the final leg of your life quietly and without complaint. I still craved change. I believed that before that death when the body gives out for one reason or another, there was another, more insidious one—the death of your sense of possibilities, a rusting of the hinges and closing of the doors inside your mind. That was the one I most feared.

And though I'd never said so aloud, I'd come to believe that Orson had appeared in my life to make sure that didn't happen. Somehow, this crazy dog next to me had become my scout. Together, we were headed somewhere.

From the crossroads at Bedlam Corners, I looked up at a hillside and saw a regal farmhouse tucked behind old trees, surrounded by faded barns and unmowed fields. From a broad front porch with rocking chairs, it had an unobstructed view of sweeping farmland and wooded valleys that rolled all the way to Vermont. I reached for the phone again.

"I like that place up on the hill," I told the Realtor.

"It's not for sale," she said.

A few weeks later, Paula and Emma and I and the dogs were vacationing on Cape Cod and the agent called. "You know your dream farm? It's on the market."

And now Orson and I were waiting for the moving van. He was drawn—obsessively, as usual—to the chipmunks darting in and out of the barn.

Along with the truck carrying the contents of our little cabin, another cargo would soon arrive: fifteen of Carolyn's ewes, because they were "dog broke," familiar with herding dogs. When the farm transport trailer pulled up, Carol the Lonely Donkey would trot off, too.

Well, I told myself, I no longer felt stuck in the rut of suburban midlife. Quite the opposite: I was terrified. "What have you done?" I asked Orson. He just tore after another chipmunk.

Orson was one of those dogs who gave unqualified love to only one living thing: me. He was also very attached to Paula and Emma and a few select people (like Carolyn), but by and large he didn't really warm to other animals or people.

He didn't often tolerate their coming near me or our house. He'd fling himself against doors, gates, and car windows to ward off intruders; his standard greeting to another dog was to charge.

Orson was fond of little Rose, but he bullied poor Homer. He wouldn't let him come within three feet of me, glowered at Homer while he ate until he abandoned his bowl and fled the room, stole his toys and bones. Homer generally took refuge in any room where Orson wasn't.

But he had surprising amounts of affection, too, sometimes reserved for the oddest of recipients.

Our second spring on Bedlam Farm, a new friend offered me a rooster named Winston and three hens, so that I would have fresh eggs. I'd been impressed by the industrious, businesslike nature of her own flock of chickens.

And Winston had a dramatic backstory, for a rooster. Speckled black and white, with a Patton-like authority, he had a bad leg, acquired in an epic battle defending his flock from a hawk. Two hens had been lost in the mayhem, but a mangled Winston had bought the others enough time to hustle inside their henhouse. He deserved an honorable retirement, and since I also limped on a bad left leg, we seemed a good fit.

When the chickens arrived, Orson—thinking lunch all

the way—took off after them. But I'd anticipated this welcome, so I had him on a long lead. And after a few days, filled
with many treats, lectures, and screams from me, he understood that these were cohabitants, not random prey. It helped
that I made a point of scattering liver treats on the ground
whenever we came near the chickens.

So I was surprised and horrified to look out my office
window one afternoon and see Winston commandeer the
front lawn and hobble, with purpose and dignity, right
toward Orson, napping in the sun. I didn't have time to get
outside and intercept Winston, so I stood watching tensely
from the window. I saw Orson's eye open like one of those
cartoon foxes or cats when a tempting mouse strolls by. Border collies are genetically close to wolves, and Orson had lots
of wolf in him. He'd chase not only chipmunks and field
mice, but deer and wild turkeys. I knocked frantically on the
window glass, hoping either to distract him or scare Winston
off.

But the rooster marched straight up the slope like Pickett
at Gettysburg—or his British namesake. If he'd had a sword,
it would have been drawn. Into the valley of the shadow, I
thought.

Orson sat up suddenly, but Winston kept coming. He's
gone, I thought, rushing toward the front door. It took me
only a few seconds, but when I got out onto the porch, I saw
Winston seat himself next to Orson, who was now staring at
the rooster in amazement. Orson's ears were up, and his tail
was twitching, neither of which I took to be a good sign.
Still, Winston was alive.

Orson looked at me; I made what I hoped were soothing
noises. Then he sighed, lay back down, and resumed his
snooze.

I could hardly believe it. But over the next few days, there was no doubt: an inexplicable friendship was born.

When Orson and I came into the barn, Orson sniffed Winston, even gave him a lick once in a while. When Orson was out in the yard, Winston limped over to visit, clucking and puffing. The two pals napped together on sunny afternoons.

Maybe *pals* was an exaggeration; Winston never looked directly at Orson, just settled down comfortably beside him; Orson didn't seek Winston out, but accepted his presence. I often glanced out the living room window and marveled at the sight of these two creatures, both staring out over the valley, each seemingly lost in his own thoughts but content to ponder things together. Orson was not a meditative creature by nature. This friendship—or whatever it was—was good for him, I decided.

The relationship only ripened. When a stray dog came running up the road after the chickens, Orson rushed protectively in front of Winston and, barking furiously, drove the rattled intruder off. When Orson and I took walks up into the pasture, Winston often started up the hill with us. Like me, he couldn't go far or fast, so he rarely made it up to the crest of the hill in time. But once in a while, if we stayed up there long enough, he joined us. I had some happy moments sitting up there in an Adirondack chair with my strange dog and his new buddy, all of us taking in the sunshine and the scenery.

It's healthy to remember, dealing with dogs and other animals, that we are largely ignorant. There were parts to this dog that I would never understand.

For instance:

If Orson could befriend, or at least tolerate, a grumpy rooster, why was he so hostile to gentle, enthusiastic service and therapy dogs? It seems an odd thing to say, but over time, it simply became clear: He didn't like exuberant, social dogs like Labs and golden retrievers. He didn't like Seeing Eye dogs. He didn't like puppies. Almost any dog that made people go "awwww" just set him off.

The strange thing about this trait was, I loved him for it. Service and therapy dogs and their owners do great work; they deserve praise and appreciation. But in the same way the official class bad boy often resents the overachievers, Orson disliked nice dogs, particularly if they wore one of those stenciled vests that said "Therapy." When I was in an anthropomorphic mood, I reasoned that he disdained dogs whose circumstances allowed them to be nicer than he was. Perhaps they were the dogs he wished he could be.

One Sunday afternoon I took him to a reading in Saratoga. He loved the attention he got at book events, although applause would sometimes arouse him and spark a spate of barking.

At this store, a blind woman showed up with Maggie, her beloved Seeing Eye dog, a true sweetheart. In seconds, while I was distracted by conversation, Orson slipped his collar and was running Maggie down the aisles. I could hear barking and yelping at the far end of the store. Maggie's owner looked bewildered, calling to her dog, saying over and over, "She never runs off. Where could she be?"

Hurrying to the store entrance, I saw that Orson had chased Maggie right out the front door—while it was held open by a customer, apparently—and under a car in the mall parking lot. Maggie looked traumatized. Orson, barking and circling, appeared to be having a good time. I was mortified. What kind of miserable creature goes after a Seeing Eye dog?

"They're out here," I yelled back into the store. "They're just playing."

Then, cursing, I kneeled down and grabbed Maggie's halter. Orson, chastened by my tongue-lashing, slithered along the ground. Maggie looked rattled but eager to get back to her post; owner and dog were happily reunited. Orson, after numerous muttered death threats, lay down next to me while I read and talked and signed. But he never took his eyes off Maggie.

How *do* you love a dog like that? And, more interesting, why?

People who love dogs often talk about a "lifetime" dog. I'd heard the phrase a hundred times before I came to recognize its significance.

Lifetime dogs intersect with our lives with particular impact; they're dogs we love in especially powerful, sometimes inexplicable, ways. While we may cherish other pets, we may never feel that particular kind of connection with any of the rest. For lack of a better term, they are dogs we fall in love with, and for whom we often invent complex emotional histories.

You could argue that until the end of one's life with dogs, it isn't possible to say which was your once-in-a-lifetime dog. In my experience, though, people do usually know, if they're fortunate enough to have one.

People often need to see their dogs as guarding or healing or loving them and them alone—as in the dog that pines for its owner for years, or crawls hundreds of miles across the moors to get home. I've always resisted that idea. I want my dogs to love and feel safe with others besides me. I suspect that when dogs can't, we've mistaken anxiety and confusion for love. It's not unusual for us to encourage and reinforce the behaviors we want in our dogs, then attribute our own needs and motives to them. The lifetime dog, I suspect, is an unconscious, maybe even unwilling, partner in this process.

Yet there's no denying the degree to which Orson and I bonded. He was always with me, when he could be. And I always had him with me, when I could. I even took him halfway across the country when I taught at the University of Minnesota one fall.

I worried about Orson all the time. It pained me greatly when he suffered, and I was exhilarated when he seemed happy. It felt like a pure relationship of unquestioned love, unbreakable loyalty, and the absence of judgment. Who knows whether he felt anything like this? But because he couldn't speak, I could speak for him, imagine a personality for him, whether it was accurate or not.

His spirit seemed parallel to mine. There was a link, a connection, that I couldn't explain. But I felt it nonetheless.

So when I sensed that something central in my life had changed since Orson arrived, I was right and wrong.

As I'd settled into a suburban white-collar life, almost unthinkingly, I'd drifted away from a part of myself. When Orson arrived, he began reconnecting me to that other self; it was obvious as soon as I set foot on the farm and felt such joy, fulfillment, and contentment. I doubt he did this by design. It's less awkward to speak in terms of his sparking something within me that was long dormant. Yet no other dog I ever loved could have done this, or could do it again. Orson's pain touched me; his plight inspired me; his love comforted me. When I came home and he threw himself upon me, my heart rose up. Sometimes I was so moved, I wanted to cry.

Without Orson, I would not be here. The happy and unhappy truths inherent in that realization will intrigue, plague, and haunt me to the end of my time.

On the early fall day the trailer from Pennsylvania arrived, and the sheep and donkey rushed out into the pasture toward the lush green grass, Orson and I soon followed. He was on a long leash, but when he looked at the sheep, that old gleam showed in his eyes.

"Hey," I hissed at him, not wanting the moment to be spoiled. "Settle down."

I walked him up the hill—perhaps a quarter of a mile— and then we turned and looked out over the sprawling valley below us. Hawks circled vigilantly overhead. Carol the donkey was gnawing happily on the bark of an old apple tree below, and the sheep had begun serious grazing, the trauma and discomfort of a long journey already forgotten. I leaned back into one of the Adirondack chairs I'd perched at the crest of the hill, savoring the sight.

Orson put his paw on my knee, and licked my face. I slipped the leash from his collar. He looked at me expectantly for directions, but I had none to give. I was suffused with gratitude for his having led me to this unimaginably beautiful place, the rumpled, balding grandson of impoverished Russian immigrants sitting atop an expanse that had sustained farmers decades before the first battles of the Civil War.

"You're free," I said. He froze for a moment, stared at me, then took off.

Animals free to move in their natural environments are a

beautiful and rare sight. There's little in the animal world to compare with the graceful lope of a border collie with work to do and lots of room to do it.

When border collies approach sheep, they're supposed to break wide of the flock, circling behind them to push them toward the shepherd. Orson was more prone to dashing right at the sheep, scattering them in a melee of fear and confusion. In nearly two years of trekking out to Carolyn's farm, in hundreds of contacts with sheep, he'd never managed that classic semicircular "outrun" behind them, except in empty fields away from sheep. Sometimes he would begin, but always, something inside him would snap. He'd turn directly toward the sheep, so that herding became chasing. It was Orson's plight, really: He could never quite escape himself, any more than I could.

But certain animals in certain situations can sense an occasion and enter the spirit of the moment, especially if they know and read their human companions well.

I was feeling exhilarated that day. Walking to the top of the hill—my hill—and looking down at the farm—my farm, with my newly arrived livestock—was a landmark moment. Could a dog as attached to me as Orson was fail to sense that?

Freed, he broke to the right and began a beautiful, bounding run far wide of the sheep, almost as if we were swept up in the pride and accomplishment of the moment—his moment as much as mine—and were determined to honor it.

A classic outrun, Discovery Channel stuff. I rose to my feet to see it better. He didn't look back at me, as he usually did. I kept my mouth shut, as I often don't.

He ran off the eastern fence, then down alongside it. The sheep, recognizing the old adversary they usually fled from, raised their heads and watched for a few moments. Then they began gathering into a knot. When Orson cantered below them, they turned and, as any shepherd would want them to do, began walking slowly up the hill toward me, Orson behind them.

He looked especially handsome on that September day, his lean, muscular frame racing along without any visible exertion, his glossy black and white fur shimmering. Another dog, one of the Labs, would have been panting by now, slowing after running hard in the warm sun. But Orson hardly seemed to be straining.

In a few minutes, the sheep were close to the top of the hill, grazing near me, watching him. Orson ran up alongside them to me. I dropped to my knees and shouted praise and hallelujahs.

What a breakthrough, I thought. How I wish Carolyn or Paula—or somebody—could have seen it. How much hard work had gone into this simple run, how many training sessions in the cold and heat and mud, how many bug bites and frozen toes. It was a remarkable triumph of commitment and training.

And we'd have great moments like this, I knew, on our farm, with our sheep in our pastures and hills. Wasn't this why we were here, why we had come?

I didn't suspect for a moment that he'd never do an outrun like that again. I'd never understand why.

Rose

CHAPTER THREE

The Rise of Rose

When I first saw Rose, she was clinging to her breeder's shoulder in the passenger terminal at Denver's vast international airport. A tiny black-and-white pup fresh from a quiet farm, she was trembling with fear at all the noise and commotion around her.

And her day was only going to get worse. She was soon stuffed into a fabric animal holder, electronically wanded and groped by airport security, then jammed into a small carry-on crate pushed beneath my airplane seat, headed for New Jersey. The crate, airline personnel repeatedly warned me, could not be opened during the flight.

I could only imagine what four or five hours of roaring jet engines were doing to so sensitive a dog. When nobody was looking, I leaned down, unfastened the container, and stroked her quivering head.

When we arrived in Newark, the din of suburban New Jersey—sirens, traffic, power mowers, people—unnerved her further. The first time I took her out into the backyard, she burrowed into an opening under the fence and wouldn't budge. I had to pull her out.

For days she cowered, rushing outside to hide among the garden greenery and peer out, then darting back inside to take refuge in her crate. She didn't eliminate for a good twenty-four hours. She was all nerves, hypersensitive to sound and movement around her, so anxious that I worried she might suffer permanent trauma of some kind. After a few days, she settled a bit and began paying a little attention to me and the other dogs. She seemed to feel safer. Still, I wondered whether a dog as anxious as this could ever herd sheep.

Rose spent her first months in New Jersey, from which base we made frequent treks out to the sheep in Pennsylvania. Then came time for the big move. I took three border collies to the farm—Rose, Homer, and Orson.

Homer was sweet-tempered and affectionate, but struggling with Orson's intensity and dominance, as well as my own impatience and inexperience with training. I'd hoped that introducing a new puppy would bolster his confidence, his position in the pack; it wasn't working out that way.

In New Jersey he had grown attached to Max, my neighbors' ten-year-old. The rest of the family adored him as well. In that household, he had plenty of attention and no trouble from competitors. While Homer's visits there had been brief, I suspected even then that one day he would stay. A lovelier setting upstate couldn't resolve his problems.

But the new puppy was instantly transformed. On the farm, Rose had come home.

She was more peaceful and at ease than I'd ever seen her, especially after the sheep arrived. It was as if she'd been born here. In New Jersey, she was a dog out of her element; on the farm, she'd found her place.

It was intriguing to see how the dogs took to this new environment, or didn't. Orson, thorny as ever, had varied responses. He loved walking with me, running through the woods and meadows, chasing chipmunks and digging into groundhog holes. But he seemed most at ease alone with me, inside the farmhouse.

Homer rarely seemed comfortable on the farm. The running and herding seemed to tire him; he often ended the day limping and sore. He was shorter than Orson and his frame heavier than Rose's, so running took more of a toll on him.

He still gave a wide berth to Orson, who rarely let him near me. Having absorbed this lesson, Homer became the only dog I'd ever owned who didn't usually want to be in the same room with me.

Curiously, Rose was completely unafraid of Orson; she deferred to him but was unrattled. In fact, at night, when all the dogs were settled, Rose tiptoed around the house collecting everybody's bones, toys, and rawhide remnants, ferrying them, piece by piece, to her own crate. She rarely chewed them, but she liked to collect them, one last round of work before sleep. She was the only dog who could take anything of Orson's and escape a drubbing.

When it came to Homer, she was as dominant as Orson. Soon, the poor guy had two dogs pushing him around, stealing his bones and toys.

My dog life had been fluid lately, to say the least. Homer had come to fill the ache after Julius and Stanley died, to be part of my growing interest in herding. Rose, descended from a strong herding line, had come to help with the farm I was about to acquire and to be a good-natured companion for Homer to feel superior to. Little of this was unfolding as planned.

In the fall, despite pangs of loss and guilt, I gave Homer to Max and his family, where he still lives happily. And little Rose practically took over.

Rose was the opposite of a mellow Lab. Aware of every sound and movement, almost incapable of relaxing, she never stopped working—moving things around, darting back and forth along the pasture fence, keeping track of me—even when she wasn't on duty. She was interested in people only as they related to work. If you walked into the pasture with her and let her steer the sheep, even once, then you were her friend. Otherwise, she had no use for you. She had scant interest in being scratched, cuddled, or hugged. Food mattered little. Apart from those that involved chasing, like balls and Frisbees, neither did toys.

If she never was quite at rest, she seemed cheerful and content. And why not? How many border collies had a score of sheep just outside the kitchen window?

My plan was to work rigorously with Orson every day—rain, snow, heat, or cold—and to raise Rose as a working farm dog, which I suspected I would soon need.

I'd bought Bedlam Farm for many reasons, some having little to do with dogs. But one factor important to me was the chance to live and work with dogs in the right environment, without suburban restrictions and distractions, with meadows and pastures and sheep.

Orson had been somehow damaged in his early years; I hoped that working together, he and I could repair much of that damage, if not all of it. That was the goal, perhaps the fantasy.

I would keep working with him until the world made sense; he would love and trust me and, in the process, heal. He wouldn't suffer the fate of so many troubled creatures— to be abandoned. Somebody would be there. Somebody would care. We wouldn't give up on each other.

Training with Orson had to be consistent, not something we did when I had time but something we did every single day, something built into our lives together. It would take a lot of work. We would keep at it until we had gone as far as we could go.

The most serious training occurred first thing in the morning. I left the other dogs inside the house or in the backyard fence, while Orson and I made for the pasture gate. He understood early on that this meant we'd be working together; it had become a part of the day that he looked forward to with excitement. When I unlatched the gate, he exploded, rushing around in circles, barking and scarfing up sheep poop, spooking the donkeys and sending the sheep to the farthest corner of the pasture. To overcome even one of these unwanted reactions—the circling, the noise, the unpleasant snacking, which had even more unpleasant consequences later in the day—would be a triumph.

Our work didn't proceed steadily and predictably, not ever. One morning in the late fall, the sheep were gathered near the feeder, waiting. It was growing bitter, and the animals needed corn and grain for energy. So I went into the barn with Orson and poured grain into two black rubber buckets.

Delivering it wasn't as simple a procedure as it might seem. Normally placid ruminants, sheep turn wild when they see or smell food. They'll plow into one another—and anything else in the way, including people—to get to grain. I had one bad leg, and worsening troubles with the other, and more than once I'd been banged into, knocked over, nearly trampled by charging sheep. On a few occasions it had been seriously frightening; it was often painful. The better approach was to keep the animals back until you could place their food in a feeder, then step away.

Orson, I thought, would be good at this. The sheep were afraid of him, understandably, and would stay away. He didn't need to execute any moves; he could simply stay near me. I opened the pasture gate and he came in, excited, expectant.

A good rule to follow with sheep and border collies, I've learned, is that a dog too excited to hear you, or obey simple commands like "Lie down," is probably too excited to work.

My training practice is to remove an overwrought dog until he calms down, then bring him back once he's settled. That way, the dog learns that he'll get to sheep when he's calm, not frenzied. I had been working on this with Orson for more than two years, and this morning I made him lie down outside the gate, and then lie down again once we came inside.

The sheep were bleating, edging closer to me and the buckets. I told Orson to lie down, and then to stay. He had rushed up looking for sheep poop, but after I'd called him two or three times, he came back and lay down.

Then I trudged uphill to the feeder with the two heavy buckets. It had been frigid for days, alternately snowing and then, when the temperature warmed up, sleeting. Now the icy ground was treacherous, even for people with two good legs.

This was a case where training blends with need. I wanted Orson to be calm. I needed him to be calm. In the back of my mind lurked the human tendency to believe that because something was important to me, Orson would—as in a Disney movie—figure it out and help me. He'd think something like this: I love Jon. Jon is about to get trampled by some sheep. I have to protect him because he has bad legs and he needs me.

Which was a good example of the way I sometimes put him in an impossible position, asking more than he could possibly give, then blaming him for failing. Dogs, like people, are often prisoners, not masters, of their instincts. Orson did love me, did want to please me, but there were other forces at work.

As I headed up the slope, Orson bolted and headed for the sheep. But corn overcomes fear in most cases where sheep are concerned. Once he moved, they moved in. With the ram, Nesbitt, leading the way, the flock slid and ran down the slope, plowing right into me. My feet went out from under me, my head banged onto frozen ground, and corn and grain went flying, sending the animals into further frenzy.

I cursed and yelled and began swinging the now-empty buckets at the sheep to push them away. My head throbbed. Orson, frantic, grabbed one of the ewes by her wool and began pulling her up the hill, puffs of fleece trailing behind. This was not a rescue effort but a freestyle freakout that had little to do with me.

I threw one of the buckets in his direction, and he was startled as it banged on the ground. "No, no, no!" I yelled.

"Get out of here. Get out!" I was furious. His behavior had injured and endangered me, and had almost harmed an animal. Now some of the sheep were scarfing up the fallen corn, and some were running from him.

I calmed down, called him to me, took him into the house and, tossing in a biscuit, put him in his crate. He seemed eager to go in, nervous and confused. After such episodes, Orson often had an air of anxious bewilderment, as if he wasn't sure what had happened. It was almost as if he'd come to, after a seizure. Perhaps he had.

I let Rose out the door, and she raced to the pasture gate and waited for me. She circled until the sheep were in a tight group, then walked them back up the hill. Limping and muttering, I refilled the buckets. I gave Rose no commands, and she wasn't looking for any. Patrolling back and forth, she simply held the sheep in place—all of them eyeing the refilled buckets—until I dumped the corn into the feeder. Then I backed away and released her, and the sheep came down the hill and ate.

"Okay, Rose, thanks and out," I said softly—almost all my commands were homegrown, not official trial jargon. She darted to the gate and we went back to the house.

I changed tactics. We took to entering the pasture with the sheep in the training pen (courtesy of Rose) and Orson on a leash. I'd release him and remain absolutely still and quiet while he ran in circles, gobbled up donkey droppings, and ran from the barn to the feeder. Sometimes it took five minutes, sometimes ten, but he would eventually look up to see where I was.

Then we walked to the pen where the sheep were, and I said, "Orson, go around." He stopped, spun, barked, and then, after a few moments, he would circle the pen in beautiful, loping runs, then turn and come back to me. I would erupt with joy, give him treats, hug and praise him effusively.

It became our daily training ritual, the thing he could do, the work he could be successful at—and, as it turned out, the outer limits of his capabilities as a herding dog.

Sometimes he got the notion of "come bye"—running around the sheep to the right while they were in the pen. Once in a while, he'd even grasp "away to me," and would break off to the left, circling the pen. But usually he'd get too excited, spinning and barking, heading off in random directions. So I just let him run around the pen without any commands, in whatever direction he wanted to go.

Every few weeks, I opened the gate and tried to get him to walk calmly behind the sheep, driving them out into the pasture. It rarely worked.

Working with Orson, in a formal sense, was endlessly frustrating. His arousal often overtook his comprehension of even the most elemental commands. For five or six days in a row, he might reliably lie down and stay. Then suddenly he'd lose it and tear around the pasture as if he'd never heard a phrase like "lie down."

After a few months, I gave up on the idea that Orson could ever work directly with sheep, unless there was a fence between them. I called this our minimalist training: stop doing too much, asking too much, expecting too much. Less is more. Simple is better. Patience is critical, praise, essential. Sometimes good enough is good enough. Sometimes—*when* is a fine and debatable point—you just have to accept and love the dog you have, even if he's not necessarily the dog you want him to be. Herding sheep isn't the only way for a border collie to be happy.

The contrast was striking, and over time, sad. Rose had the innate ability to understand the task at hand and get it done.

Like any young border collie, she needed to be taught how to stay calm and move slowly; she couldn't be allowed to run amok. But she'd arrived with most of the instinct she needed; all I had to do was give her time and reinforcement. Orson, on the other hand, had suffered the misfortune of so many dogs: He had gotten involved with humans.

Rose's behavior with the sheep was measured and authoritative. She never used her mouth to control them; she used her body and intense "eye," the stare border collies employ to move sheep and intimidate other animals, and the sheep moved as she directed.

After the first few weeks, I could simply say, "Go get the sheep," and Rose would rocket up the hill, give the herd the eye, square off for a few moments with the ram, and get behind the herd. Then—there was never any doubt of the outcome—she and the flock would come trotting down the hill and into the pen.

She was all business, undistractable, energetic and fearless. As my father often said during his fruitless efforts to turn me into a baseball player, "You've got to keep your eye on the ball." Rose did.

This was the difference, I thought, between a dog who had been given the opportunity to learn and grow safely and properly, and a dog who hadn't. It was wonderful to work with Rose, sad to see the excitable wreck that Orson, in some ways, had become.

I had thought Rose would learn some things from Orson, from the herding dog I was sure he could become, once sheep were living out the back door. But after the first few weeks, the truth seemed increasingly evident: We were all learning from Rose; none of us had much to teach her.

With little training at all, she was evolving into a cracker-jack farm dog—eager, bright, savvy, and profoundly useful.

"Where's Rose?" the large-animal vet would say when she pulled up in her pickup. Lots of her clients brought their dogs out to work when she arrived, she told me, but only Rose actually helped, keeping sick sheep still, rounding up runaways trying to avoid their shots. I nearly burst with pride.

Rose was one of those working dogs completely at ease on the job, though never completely relaxed otherwise. She was as comfortable backing up a big, bullying ram as she was out of place in New Jersey. It was hard to reconcile this busi-nesslike, energetic creature with the trembling puppy I had toted from Denver.

Our training evolved. I decided against hiring a herding instructor or taking her to a class. I decided to let her gifts de-velop naturally and see what happened.

I did a lot of things the herding instructors recom-mended—initially brought her near sheep on a leash, for in-stance, to discourage running around. But I also did a lot of things they didn't recommend, like letting her into the pas-ture alone. I watched from the gate as she approached the sheep, her eye and her instincts sharpening almost daily. She wasn't a dog to race around willy-nilly; she always seemed to have a purpose.

Most mornings, she would rush halfway up the hill—the flock had almost always drifted up to the top for the night—and take in the situation. She looked to the right, then the left, surveying the scattered sheep, until she reached some sort of conclusion. This was critical, an Irish friend and herding guru had cautioned me. "You stay quiet and let her make some decisions."

Via e-mail and telephone calls, other trainers conveyed their disapproval. "There's a right way and a wrong way to herd sheep," one trainer scolded. "You need lessons—you'll mess her up."

But working with Rose was a great experience. I'm happy we did it our own way.

Each morning, after mulling the situation, Rose moved one way or the other, quickly or slowly, to gather the flock and bring it down to me. She carried in her head a manual of some sort that showed how things ought to work. I didn't have one, so I decided to trust her and her burgeoning instincts. Her evolution was a beautiful thing to see.

Rose was too young to herd sheep—yet she *was* herding sheep. She was too young to stay calm, but she did. One couldn't expect this still-gawky pup to control animals that towered over her, including a donkey that could pulverize her with a single kick. But she did.

She was as calm as Orson was excited, as dauntless as he was convinced he would fail. As needy as he was of my presence and attention, Rose was almost indifferent to it. Working with her, I could see the enormous blocks that had been created in him—his excitement, confusion, aversion to commands, hyperarousal.

Daily her confidence grew, her experience mounted. She was poised, assured, and you could see how proud she felt after our work was done and she trotted out the pasture gate, pausing to wag her tail and give my hand a quick lick.

Day by day, she became more of a working dog, and Orson became less of one, more of a pet.

We were all still settling in at the farm when the first real blizzard of the winter struck. The wind began to shriek as sheets of snow started blowing across the yard and the road. I cranked up my new woodstove and took out a bottle of Glenlivet. The dogs were inside, curled up for the night—until Rose began barking. When I looked out the window, I saw that the donkey and the sheep had escaped through the pasture gate, crossed the road, and were vanishing off into the woods.

I panicked. I'd never been confronted with a livestock breakout before. I didn't relish having to call Paula to tell her all my animals had vanished in the storm.

It was ungrateful of them to have bolted, I thought, after I'd so carefully supplied plenty of hay and fresh water and shelter. Perhaps something spooked them. Maybe I hadn't latched the gate. In any event, there were acres and acres of forest out there. I had no way of finding the sheep, of bringing them back.

Orson was of no use in this predicament. If we did manage to locate the animals, they would just run farther at the sight of him. Rose looked at me eagerly with her send-me-in-coach look. We headed outside. "Go get 'em, girl," I yelled, having little choice. The puppy—at this point barely six months old—disappeared into the woods.

A half hour later, huffing and puffing, cursing the cold and snow and yearning for that warm fire and glass of scotch back at the farmhouse, I followed the sounds of barking off in the deep woods. When I stumbled to where she was, I saw in my flashlight's beam that she had rounded up the whole gang—sheep, ram, and donkey.

Nobody was going anywhere, as she barked, circled, and nipped. In an open forest, Rose was the fence.

She maneuvered behind the animals and, with me leading the procession, we marched them down a long path, through the meadow, and back across the road. I closed the gate behind them, piling trash cans and boards against it for good measure.

Rose, clearly, had found her destiny. All the things I had been working so hard with Orson to do were things she did naturally, instinctually. No longer the novice, she was maturing into the Queen of Bedlam, while the notion of Orson's ever being a working dog—something important to me, and, I believed, to him—began to fade. Perhaps something in his proud, needy spirit perished as well.

Rose knew without coaching how to separate the donkeys (soon there were two, later three) from the sheep. She guarded the gate if it swung open, halted the sheep at the road if we were crossing to graze. During lambing season, she alerted me when lambs were born, kept mothers and babies together while they bonded, marched ewes and their newborns into the barn where they'd be dry and warm.

Soon, other farmers were calling to borrow her for particularly demanding tasks. We put down barnyard riots, herded errant goats, held roaming cows at bay. We charged ten dollars for house calls, and before long a couple of hundred dollars had accumulated in the basket on my desk, money destined for dog-rescue groups.

We became partners in the oldest, most traditional, way of dogs and humans. Living with Rose, I understood why dogs had been domesticated in the first place. I was acutely conscious of what a dog like her might have meant to a farmer a century ago.

Something elemental had changed. Border collies need work, and Orson was intensely eager to find it. As Carolyn had predicted, and as I knew too well, the world would not make sense to him until he did.

But when he did, it wasn't the kind of work one saw border collies doing on cable shows or at herding trials. Orson's work became me. And that had to be enough.

Equilibrium came to the farm slowly that first year. The weather soon grew harsh and bleak. I had little understanding of how to manage feed, hay, and water in upstate New York's worst winter in forty years. I was overwhelmed by the physical brutality of our daily routines.

Carol, the donkey, fell gravely ill, necessitating many late-night walks to the barn with syringes and salves. I had to administer shots and pills and wrap bandages. Hauling corn and grain to the ewes, dragging hoses across the icy tundra that was my driveway so the flock would have water, lugging fifty-pound bales of hay up the hill—I found it challenging, enthralling, battering. I'd foolishly mistimed the arrival of my ram, Nesbitt, so that the ewes gave birth in February, most of them in the middle of the night, invariably in sub-zero temperatures.

Yet as my new responsibilities turned daily life upside down, Orson achieved a certain steadiness that had always eluded him. Probably it wasn't easy for him to watch Rose and me enter the pasture without him. It wasn't an easy thing for me, either. He always wanted to come with me—everywhere—so he ran to the door. Excluded, he then sat at the window, watching, waiting until I returned.

But he found compensations. The farm was quiet in the

winter, with few visitors and distractions. I still worked with him each morning, but we simply went out to the pasture, and after he circled the pen a few times, I showered him with praise. He was feeling successful, I thought, or at least feeling like a failure less often.

With deadlines looming and the bitter weather discouraging roaming, I felt less guilty than normal about holing up inside to work. I noticed that Orson came to see my work as his responsibility, too. When the computer hummed to life, he plopped down on the floor next to me, his head often resting on my right foot. Soon he would sigh deeply and go to sleep.

Rose loved to sit out in the yard on the bitterest days, so she could keep an eye on her sheep. She had no interest in my work, only hers. Sometimes, when I went out to call her, Rose was nearly invisible, covered with snow. She popped up out of the whiteness, shook herself off, and rushed into the house—straight through to the back door, hoping to go back outside and collect some sheep. She would happily have lived outside, the better to guard her flock.

Orson was different, and perhaps we were all becoming more comfortable with that. I appreciated his companionship through that awful winter. His time with me by the computer, as the woodstove crackled, became our work together. I loved having him so close as I wrote. Often, because I didn't want to disturb him, my leg ached from keeping it so still.

A soulful, peaceful side of him emerged that had been harder to see out in Carolyn's pasture or back in New Jersey. While I clacked away at the keyboard, this once restless creature would lie contentedly for hours. If I reached down to stroke or pat him, he licked my hand, met my eyes, thumped his tail a couple of times, then went back to sleep. In this way, day after day, we wrote a book together.

His newfound peacefulness was infectious. Once again, I marveled at the diverse, complex nature of dogs, the myriad ways in which they work their way into our hearts. Whenever I looked down at Orson, I smiled.

To own such a dog is not, as many readers know, a simple thing. It requires vigilance and spawns anxiety. Will he take off after some poor dog walking down the road? Break through the screen door after a chipmunk? Terrorize the oil deliveryman? One could rarely relax around a dog like Orson, yet that winter, in my office, as the temperatures outside plummeted and the winds whistled, I did relax, and so, I think, did he. He had found work he loved to do, that he was very good at. The next six months were the most peaceful, I think, of Orson's complicated life.

When spring finally came, we took several walks through the day, sometimes into the woods, sometimes down to Black Creek for a swim. He tore through the meadow, diving for field mice and moles, rolling in deer scat, erupting in joyous bursts of energy. He rarely had much to do with sheep, but he didn't seem to care. Neither did I. Finally, the pressure seemed to lift a bit. He was content.

He was even gracious to—or at least tolerant of—little Clementine, my sweet-faced new Lab puppy.

I'm very partial to border collies. I love their intensity, intelligence, and affection, the energy they exude and demand from their humans. But I missed having Labs. Julius and Stanley were as delightful and affable companions as I'd ever had. I wanted a simple dog, one happy to hang around, doze at my feet, watch a Yankees game.

So I pestered Pam Leslie, a highly regarded breeder in Vermont, until she told me about a litter that included a couple of yellow Labs. Then I pestered her to sell me one.

Clementine was pure Labrador: nothing was too disgusting for her to gobble up; she rarely took offense; she loved most living things, including sheep and donkeys. Orson did not play, and had little patience for dogs that did, but he took a lot of stuff from Clem, who grabbed his biscuits and chewbones, tore through the house annoying him, and vied shamelessly for my affection. Once or twice he growled a warning to get away, but generally he seemed amused and never intimidated her the way he had Homer.

Clem loosened the place up, getting Rose to play hide-and-seek once in a while. She even got Orson to relax. She and I were soon watching baseball together on the sofa, Clem stretched out next to me, snoring through the innings. She was a lovely addition.

The only trouble we had was when somebody came to visit—delivery person or friend, it didn't seem to matter much—and Orson hurled himself almost hysterically at the door or gate.

But otherwise, he appeared—for him—at ease. Perhaps we're finally getting it, I thought.

Orson had friends, almost all of them female. His girlfriends, I called them—dog lovers, neighbors, and friends who adored Orson. They knew him as an affectionate, playful, and relentlessly social creature prone to crawling into their laps; he had a charming, almost flirtatious, mode with women.

An attention addict, he loved being the center of things; if attention didn't flow naturally, he was a genius at getting people—especially me—to focus on him.

But he didn't have to work hard for attention from his

girlfriends, who cooed and fussed over him. His tail started wagging the second he heard their trucks. They brought him treats, brushed his coat until it gleamed, had long conversations with him. When he was not around sheep, doors, or gates, Orson could be pretty sociable. "You are a slut," I would mutter, as his girlfriends left.

A dog can be a pussycat at home, a rampaging monster outside. How do you explain to a terrified FedEx driver that the dog lunging and barking at him might be the creature that's loved you more faithfully than any other?

I was constantly interpreting for Orson, with his multiple personalities. *He's really a sweetheart, it's just that border collies bark and nip. He's a good guy, he doesn't really hurt people, it's just a boundary problem.* I appreciated the girlfriends, not only because they were my friends, but because I never had to explain. They saw the same Orson that I knew; they, too, loved him for his vulnerability, for having a great heart despite a confused life.

Sometimes, even strangers could see that in Orson. A woman in the nearby town of Granville called me one afternoon to say that she'd read about him in *A Dog Year,* a book about our first year together. Catherine had come up from Westchester to stay with her mother, who was gravely ill. Although she hated to ask, she wondered whether I might bring Orson by for a visit. Her mother had enjoyed reading about him, was eager to meet him, and could no longer get around much.

"He's not always gentle," I warned her. "He can get excited sometimes." But she said she and her mother, Madeline, would take the chance.

Madeline's husband had been a dairy farmer until his

death five years earlier. She had remained on the farm as long as she could, but Madeline's days there were numbered. She was failing.

I'd developed a soft spot for farmers. Many of my friends now were farmers, and I was moved by how hard they struggled, and how doomed their way of life seemed. There was no way I could say no.

We drove up that same afternoon. The farm was off Route 22, perhaps fifteen miles from me, four miles north of the only McDonald's for miles.

Decaying trucks and tractors, cannibalized for engine parts—the signature lawn ornaments of the dying family farm—littered the drive. Two giant barns, empty and neglected, were both tottering visibly. A few chickens pecked in the yard, but we saw no other animals. Catherine, an attractive woman in her forties, met us at the farmhouse door and showed us in.

The house smelled of cats and sickness. Madeline, sitting in an armchair in the living room, had wispy white hair; a cotton sweater hung on her tiny, birdlike frame.

She spoke in the sad, reflective tone of someone who knew that time was short. "I was hoping to make it to Florida for a few years," she said, after apologizing for the house. "But I think I'm headed for a nursing home instead. I hoped to die on the farm, but that may not be possible."

Orson had spotted a girlfriend—any female who thought him handsome and sweet—and made a beeline to Madeline. As if they'd known each other for years, he circled to the side of her chair and offered her a paw. Then he licked her hand, and rested his head on her lap.

I started to call him off, fearing that this frail woman

couldn't handle him, but I stopped when I saw her take his head in her arms for a hug. He closed his eyes; she did, too.

They probably sat like that for just a few minutes, but it seemed like longer. "I'm afraid that this may be the last time I will ever hold a sweet dog like this," Madeline said, wiping away tears, looking embarrassed. "He is as wonderful as I knew he would be." And what could I say?

Orson and Jon

CHAPTER FOUR

The Contract

Almost from the moment Orson arrived in New Jersey, our life together was shaped by a nearly continuous series of arguments, confrontations, misunderstandings, and disputes, punctuated by great fun, love, and an ever-deepening attachment.

We disagreed over his right to chase school buses, or kids on bikes and skateboards. Or his tendency to charge after small dogs and try to herd them down the block toward me. Or his love of bursting into strangers' backyards in search of dogs, cats, and barbecuing burgers.

I did not believe it was appropriate for him to open the refrigerator with his nose, take food from plastic containers, and hide the empties under sofas. Or to plow through glass windows. Or find his way through, around, and under the picket fence in the backyard.

I felt strongly that he should not stick his nose into paper bags in the car, remove the ham or turkey from sandwiches and leave the bread.

One of our typical, often memorable, disagreements centered around a neighbor's cat that continually sassed him from the safety of a living room window, hissing and flashing her butt while he barked and yelped on a leash. One summer morning, that window was open, leaving nothing but a screen between this taunting cat and Orson. I did not agree with his decision to rush up onto the porch, leap through the screen (the resulting dog-shaped hole looked like a Wile E. Coyote cartoon), and chase the cat through the living room, over the couple sleeping in their beds, upstairs into the attic, where he cornered and terrorized the cat (but didn't hurt her), and then return via the torn screen. People said my screaming and cursing could be heard all the way down the block. I strongly expressed my differing point of view to him. This dispute cost me $500 in broken lamps and screen repair. We never saw the cat in the window again.

We quarreled over his terrorizing of Homer—he glowered Homer away from his food, then tried to steal it—or his charging and nipping of people who approached the gate, or his demented pursuit of garbage trucks and fire engines.

We had differing worldviews, he and I. He occasionally obeyed me, when it was convenient, or there was nothing more compelling to do. He was definitely one of those dogs prepared to go his own way and happily take the consequences. Obedience was, to him, a fluid notion, one of those ideas important to me but not always relevant to him. And these were explosive, powerful instincts. There was hardly a nanosecond between the time he saw something—the cat, for example—and he exploded after it. I rarely had time to move, let alone issue commands.

Our mounting quarrels culminated in a nearly literal fist-fight we had when he pushed open the front-porch screen door one morning, tore out of the house and into the street, and tried to herd yet another passing school bus. I found this obsession neither cute nor trivial: He could easily have been killed, and kids on the bus hurt by the driver's sudden braking. We'd had this fight too many times, including the time we'd run from the police.

This time I was enraged. I believed—I would perhaps view it differently now—that he understood that he was being defiant and dangerous, was purposefully thwarting me, blowing me off, rejecting my alphaness. All those training books I'd been reading said I was supposed to show him who was boss, force him to accept my authority, take charge.

At the time, I angrily collared him and dragged him inside, only to have him slip his leash and take off after another bus when I walked him half an hour later. I was tired and frustrated, sick of arguing with Orson, sick of losing. Months of these incidents caused something in me to snap, and I charged into the street, dragged him onto the sidewalk, threw him about ten feet into some shrubs, tossed the pooper scooper at him, along with my Yankees cap, and screamed that he was bad, that he must never do this again, that he could not stay with me if this was going to continue. I told him he simply could not live with me in New Jersey if something didn't change.

Orson was shocked by my raging and yelling, and frightened as well. He lay on his back with his feet in the air, a rare gesture of submission from a relentlessly dominant dog. I was nearly weeping with frustration, torn by my growing love for this dog and my growing realization that communicating with, understanding, training, and controlling him was, so far, beyond me, and was leading both of us toward trouble.

I didn't know enough about him, or about dogs. I was losing track of how many times he'd nearly killed himself or frightened and disturbed some human or dog.

During one of Paula's first walks alone with him, he'd bolted across the street and gotten hit broadside by a passing car. He bounced fifteen or twenty feet, then bounded to his feet. The vet could find nothing wrong with him.

But he couldn't live in New Jersey this way. I either had to do better or send him back to Texas. I think it was at that moment that I realized that I would never send him back, that I would do anything within reason and within my power to train him, calm him down, and keep him in my life.

I spoke to him of this that morning, as neighbors gawked at the spectacle: Orson cradled in my arms; cap, scooper, and other debris strewn about; the angry bus driver moving off, shouting warnings at me and the dog. I'd hurt Orson that morning, throwing him around like that. I'd scared him and myself, but I'd also grasped the depth of my attachment—and commitment—to him.

We can't go on this way, I explained. I've got to do better. You've got to do better. I've got to be clearer, to find a way to get through to you. You've got to hear me and stop doing crazy things that will get you or some other creature hurt.

We both began to calm down. His tail began to swish, and he kept reaching up to lick my face. I felt that I'd somehow communicated to him, shaken him up.

Out of this confrontation came the fundamental under-standing between us. I sometimes called it our covenant, or our contract, because it was in so many ways about faith and commitment, about the love that I have always wanted and needed and which he seemed to need, too. It was a significant agreement, one that was to change my life soon, in dramatic and completely unexpected ways.

Looking back, with the cheap benefit of time, it seems an arrogant, inappropriate, even absurd thing to have done. Dogs have complex and wonderful minds, but they are foreign to us in many ways. They think, but not like us. They reason, but not the way we do. They can't enter into agreements. They can't adopt our ideas of faith and propriety, can't be held responsible for our notions of commitment and responsibility, for our needs and wants.

As I sit here on the farm, that important argument—a treaty, perhaps—seems a lifetime ago. It's hard to imagine my life before Orson, now that I rise at five to walk the dogs and haul hay out to the sheep, spend my day gathering eggs and tending to a donkey's cracked hoof, and fall asleep by nine.

I'd always loved dogs, but they hovered in the background of my life. I had no reason to think about them much, until Orson came. Then they suddenly burst into the center and I was thinking about them much of the time. Orson changed the shape and order of things.

I was a prisoner and victim of my own bumbling goodwill and ignorance, and so, soon enough, was he. If I'd known then what I know now, I can't imagine entering into any kind of compact with a dog. But then, if I'd known more, I probably wouldn't have driven to Newark Airport to pick up that dog. And how much poorer I would have been.

"Here's the thing," I thought out loud and explained to Orson that morning in New Jersey as the life of the neighborhood coursed curiously around us. If people were wondering about a man lying in the ivy with a dog in his lap, they were also going about their business, heading for work or school. Many of them had been watching me chase this dog across yards and streets for months.

It was time for a change. "I will keep faith with you. I will stay committed to you. We will not quit on each other. We will not give up on each other."

I was convinced he was as committed to this understanding as I. I would do anything within reason to help him, to train him, to calm him, to guide and lead him and show him how to live in the world. He would stick it out with me, learn and grow with me, and we would be able to live together, happily and lovingly.

Things did get better after that awful fight. Orson never chased after a school bus after that morning. He did pay more attention to me, although not always. Our basic and painstaking grounding and obedience work did begin to pay off. He didn't become a different dog, but he did become a calmer one. I began to understand that my job was to lead and guide him, not to negotiate bargains with him. This did him more good.

Our arguments continued, as life on the farm presented a wide range of things to disagree about. I didn't agree with his practice of charging and nipping at gates and doors. I couldn't endorse the rough way he handled sheep. I protested his plunging into brambles and sticky burrs, his wolfing down dead animals and deer scat, his relentless persecution of Homer.

But our covenant was a turning point. If we were committed to each other, if there was no turning back, then how could my life with him fail?

It was a warm spring day at the farm. Rose, a bit worn from walking the sheep across the road and babysitting them in the meadow, was dozing in the fenced run behind the house. Clementine, my new Lab puppy, was next to her, contentedly gnawing on some rawhide. After a few weeks of growling whenever Clem came near, Rose had allowed her to sit close. (Rose did not yet deign to play—she did not play, had not ever played, something that seemed to puzzle Clementine to the core.)

Rose occasionally lifted her head up to see where the sheep were, then lay down.

Orson and I were off on a picnic, headed together up the pasture hill to the two Adirondack chairs I had positioned there. Most days, if the weather permitted, Orson and I had lunch up there. I usually made myself a sandwich, took an apple and a bottle of water in a backpack, along with a few biscuits.

We would enter the pasture—the sheep would make themselves scarce—and Orson would circle me, happy to be coming along. Like Rose, he had a conceptual streak: even if he didn't know precisely what we were doing, he got the idea. If I picked up the backpack and headed through the gate, we were going up the hill, so he would head for the gate, delighted to join in this new ritual.

If we had a favorite spot on earth, the top of the hill was probably it, although we would soon find another. The chairs were built by Don Coldwell, a master carpenter and friend who lived in the village. He also made me the beautiful ash walking stick—enscribed with the name "Bedlam Farm"—that helped steady me as we made the climb.

It was about a third of a mile from the farmhouse, and we had to climb a steep hill—I always grew a bit winded, Orson never did—then open the uppermost gate and turn left to a shady spot where the two chairs sat nestled, nearly hidden by the trees.

The walk got progressively tougher as my leg troubles increased. My knee hurt and my ankle was weak and sometimes gave way suddenly. Often, increasingly, I fell. It was a Vermont reporter visiting me who noticed that at certain points in our walks, Orson pressed close against my knee. I'd assumed he just wanted a pat, but once she asked me about it I realized that this happened at spots where I had fallen in the past. He remembered. When I did fall, he rushed over to me, frantically licked my face and gnawed at my ear until I got up. There was no way he would leave me lying there.

At such moments, he seemed especially Rin Tin Tin to me. I believed that if I stumbled and then, for any reason, couldn't get to my feet, I could turn to him and say "Orson, boy, go get help! Go get Anthony!" and he would be off like a rocket and my friend Anthony Armstrong would soon come roaring up in his pickup to save me.

I had come to view Orson as my guardian, my protector. That somehow seemed part of the deal. We would watch out for each other. Rose was an immensely better working dog, but it was Orson I turned to when I thought *I* might be in trouble—when a menacing dog appeared, when a wild pig popped out of the woods nearby and attacked Rose, when blizzards roared down from Canada, when coyotes circled up on the hill, when I needed company to hike up the hill. Orson had my back. We still had plenty of disagreements, but he was a good man in a brawl, fearless, faithful, loyal, a warrior for love.

Once we got to the top of the hill, Orson plumped down and put his head on one of my feet. I took a deep breath and looked out at the beautiful and verdant valley that spread all the way to Vermont, at the sheep grazing below, at my beautiful old farmhouse with its rich history, at the hawks circling above. I shook my head in wonder that I could claim this spot, and was nearly overwhelmed with gratitude for the dog who had somehow, in ways I had not begun to understand, led me here.

Sometimes I read or dozed in the warm breeze. This day, I just leaned over to scratch Orson's nose. We were both as peaceful up there as we ever were anywhere.

Then we made the much easier hike back down. At the bottom of the hill, I let Rose and Clem out of their fence, and the four of us walked across the road and down into the meadow, so the dogs could plunge into the stream to cool off and swim.

Orson was always the first one down the path and into the water; he loved to circle a few times like an old lady at the beach, then tear back to me. Clem chased sticks and balls, while Rose skittered across to the opposite bank to see if there was anything to herd.

Then we all marched back. It occurred to me on those walks that my time on this farm was perhaps limited. I was getting older. The farm rested on steep hills, muddy in spring, treacherously icy in winter. I sometimes felt I was drowning in the rituals and the chores of a farm. My leg throbbed when I walked uphill, and the pain could be punishing.

Bedlam Farm was a daunting place for a middle-aged man with a bum leg. But I was not alone or unprotected. Orson and I had made a good deal, and both of us were sticking to it.

Orson

CHAPTER FIVE

The Big Nipper

Chris, the FedEx man, drove many miles on the rural route he covered. He came to my farmhouse three or four times a week, bringing books and CDs, computer paraphernalia, farm and dog supplies.

He loved dogs—he had three of his own—and knew how to handle the ones he encountered. You could tell he was comfortable around them.

When his truck pulled into the driveway, right alongside the front yard and the side door to the house, Orson was likely to go berserk. But Chris, patient and experienced, got out of his truck, stepped back calmly, avoided eye contact and approached the house walking sideways, all the while talking normally, saying "Hey, Orson," and praising him when he was quiet. Usually Orson was not quiet. But he did love food, and when Chris reached into his pocket for a biscuit, the barking paused. Then Chris would toss the treat over the dog's shoulder.

The idea was to calm Orson, to reward him for being calm, and to steer his attention away from the truck and from Chris. Meanwhile, when I heard the barking, I walked outside to get the packages and put Orson on a leash. Next to me, and away from the doorway, Orson settled down. When he was calm, Chris tossed Orson another treat, and soon Orson would accept pats and scratches and lick Chris's hand. It usually took two or three minutes for Orson to cool off enough to be trusted. Then I removed the leash, and he sniffed affably around the truck.

Chris and I took this calming and acclimating ritual seriously. Over the course of six months, Chris would probably be here nearly a hundred times. If we stuck with it, we agreed, Orson would accept the presence of the truck and its driver. Enough introductions, dog biscuits, scratches, and hugs and Orson would get the idea. He'd become desensitized to the truck, welcome Chris, and perhaps be more comfortable with others as well.

One spring day—Chris guesses it might have been his seventieth or eightieth delivery—Orson didn't bark when the FedEx truck pulled into the driveway, just sat still, wagging his tail. I was in the barn, doing chores.

Chris got out and tossed Orson the usual biscuit; he scarfed it up and walked over quietly, his tail going more rapidly, his ears up. He seemed to recognize Chris instantly, and was focused on his hand—the source of treats.

Chris, pleased, thought he'd broken through. He reached over slowly, tossing biscuits every few seconds. Orson ate the biscuits, turned, and nipped the thumb of Chris's right glove, tearing it nearly off. There was no blood, no injury, just astonishment.

"I really thought we had it," Chris said.

Border collies sometimes do nip—people, animals, balls, anything that moves rapidly away from them. This is a natural behavior, the way they control large animals and induce them to go where they want them to. When people like me get a dog like Orson, they tend immediately to demand that the dog eliminate its natural behaviors and live the way humans prefer. Inevitably there's some tension. In fact, there can be civil war.

I saw the fight in New Jersey as our personal Appomattox, a kind of truce. Much later, I recognized it as only the first of a number of turning points. I kept wanting to declare our personal struggle over, proclaim myself victorious, and leave the field of battle. Of course, the skirmishing had just begun.

Orson did appear to focus on me more, for whatever reason, after that tussle. He more readily accepted my authority, or at least the idea of it. Yet our new understanding didn't spell the end of the long, uphill battle this dog faced to subordinate his nature to human expectations.

Tens of millions of dogs make this accommodation every day. Lots don't, often with sad consequences, and the more powerful the instincts, or damaged the dog, the tougher the struggle.

Border collies often upset their people primarily because they're supposed to be a smart breed; their owners don't recognize that they're also intense, instinctive, even odd creatures. If you don't have work for them, they will find some on their own; odds are, it won't be the kind of work you want done. We think of these dogs herding sheep, but their own definitions of work are much more fluid.

Orson, for example, didn't like where I kept the magazines that streamed weekly into the house in New Jersey. He decided to move them. Every time I glanced up, he was skittering up or down the staircase with a recent *Newsweek* or *Rolling Stone* in his mouth. Paula and I kept magazines in a pile downstairs, where we could skim through them in the evening. Orson, however, felt they should be upstairs, by the bed.

This was a perfect job for an obsessive dog looking to keep busy. I scolded Orson when I caught him, and put the magazines back on the stack, but I couldn't make much of a dent in this new routine. After a couple of months, we began reading magazines in bed.

Border collies generally shouldn't use their mouths when working. But I learned that there are times—say, dealing with rebellious ewes, obstreperous rams, and grumpy donkeys—when nipping becomes an essential tool. A good herder will not bite a sheep, but might "pull some wool" once in a while.

Rose has nipped cows to get them moving, and backed up rams by nipping them on the nose; it sometimes proves an invaluable work tool, even a matter of survival. Now and then, two or three ewes get it into their heads that they don't feel like moving across the road to graze, or they want to flee the shearer, or the vet. Rose convinces them otherwise, sometimes by discreetly nipping their noses or butts.

Sometimes sheep get tired or hot. Sometimes they feel protective of their lambs. Sometimes they're just ticked off. They will kick, butt, or run away, struggles that a working dog like Rose quickly learns she must win, by any means. So, many border collies will nip now and then.

Orson was a nipper—the Big Nipper, I started calling him. In New Jersey, where there were significantly more people per square mile, he sometimes nipped at people who grabbed him too enthusiastically about the face or tail, or at people who edged too close to our backyard gate. He nipped garbage trucks if he could.

And at times he was more than a nipper. When highly aroused, he could grow crazed, barking and lunging, not completely under my control or his own. Every dog owner has his own definitions, but I consider a dog potentially dangerous if he or she cannot be recalled instantly, 100 percent of the time. Orson couldn't.

Yet he seemed to go in cycles. Sometimes the arousal got better, sometimes it got worse. I was always celebrating the former, then despairing over the latter, always right and always wrong.

But if Orson was a pain, he was a manageable one. In New Jersey, where life went from chaotic to mundane, whole weeks would pass without incident. We went for long walks through the neighborhood, trekked out to Raspberry Ridge for lessons, met other dogs and dog lovers at local parks.

This is where guilt and responsibility often collide with a dog like this: Orson should almost always have been leashed, crated, or kenneled, at least until he was fully and completely trained. I knew, even then, that most border collies can't really live fully or happily in a place like suburban New Jersey. That's part of why I bought a farm.

Yet before then, Orson needed more, to my mind, and I was determined to give it to him. He needed a lot of exercise, so I took him to run in parks at five a.m. when no one much was around. He needed to explore things, so I walked him off-leash at odd hours, when commuters weren't rushing about and kids weren't heading to school. Usually this worked out fine. Sometimes he got into trouble, and the fault was mine, not his.

Like his owner, Orson was rife with contradictions. He exhibited great sweetness and true craziness, in almost equal parts. Orson liked women, of almost all ages, any shape or size or color. What he did not like was anyone coming through what I call transition points—doors, gates, fences. He didn't much like men. He didn't like men wearing dark clothing. He especially didn't like men wearing dark clothes and carrying tools.

I don't know whether these aversions stemmed from some atavistic border collie herding behavior, from a tendency toward hyperarousal, from an overdeveloped territoriality, or from plain insanity.

One afternoon in New Jersey, a landscaper walked by carrying a rake. Orson leaped up without warning and began biting the rake, trying to pull it out of the guy's hand; the poor man dropped the rake and ran. What was this about? Had someone once hit Orson with a rake? Did he think it his job to keep people with sticks away from me?

I didn't know. I would never know.

Orson loved kids, but where did he acquire a visceral loathing of lunch boxes? He loved strollers, nosing around behind the babies for food. He was drawn to anyone in a wheelchair and was very fond of older people, seeking them out, charming them, nuzzling their hands. "What a love," they would say. "What a sweetie!" Fifteen minutes later, some teenaged skateboarder would be running for his life. There is a big difference between nipping and biting, but it's a distinction that's often (understandably) meaningless to the recipient. It's no excuse for my dog to nip somebody because he's a border collie. I have to be aware that a dog like Orson may nip fast-moving things, and take the necessary precautions.

I sometimes forgot what Orson illustrated so dramatically—that dogs have alien minds, often beyond our understanding.

On the farm there were different cycles, new realities.

That first year, we were alone much of the time, especially in bitter winter. Days would pass without anybody much coming by the farm, which allowed Orson, for perhaps the first time, to settle into a calm routine. There were just fewer things around to fire him up, fewer people, trucks, dogs, sirens. He got to work out his aggression, or defensiveness—whatever it was—by tearing around the woods several times a day, wearing himself out.

Orson's outbursts were reckless. He plowed into a tree while running down a chipmunk, cracked his leg (two fractures) leaping over stone walls, sliced his paw on some ancient barbed wire still lurking in the woods. But he liked his creature comforts, too. On bitter, snowy days, he was happy to curl up indoors while I worked, whereas Rose would happily sit outside in a blizzard until she became a featureless mound in the snow.

My friend Anthony, who perhaps knew Orson better than anyone upstate besides Paula and me, loved Orson dearly, but approached him carefully. He understood Orson's crossed wires.

Country kids often have to run from roaming dogs, though they can't always run fast enough. They tend to respect dogs' natures, while city dwellers and suburbanites seem more likely to forget that their dogs are animals.

So Anthony knew that Orson might try to nip him if he reached his hand over the kennel fence or walked into the house, no matter how much Orson appeared to recognize him or how many times Anthony said his name. He would come in, saying, "Orson, Orson, get back." Sometimes he tossed a biscuit in first, to distract Orson and calm him down. Orson seemed to regain control of himself and come over to Anthony for a pat.

Joking with Anthony about Orson's nipping, I began to research the legal definition of a dog bite. In most states, I learned, a "bite" requires penetration, either of flesh or clothing. Nips, on the other hand, generally are not considered bites if they cause no damage and leave no marks.

"He bit me!" Anthony would shout on those occasions that Orson took off after him. "No," I said. "He nipped you. Under the law, he hasn't bitten anybody." This was joking banter, yet it was also an excuse I was talking myself into, a way of avoiding my fears about this dog.

I was hiding behind technicalities, insisting that a nip was unpleasant but more or less natural for the breed, while a bite was different, something other dogs did—so I reassured myself. Until, one day, one of my neighbors came by. He wanted me to know that Orson had lunged at him and torn the cuff of his sweatshirt. He showed me the shredded sleeve.

What happened? I asked, alarmed.

He'd come to the back door, and Orson had charged the gate of his backyard kennel, barking furiously. The guy had reached over to calm and pet Orson, whom he'd previously met several times, and was stunned when Orson lunged and tore his sweatshirt. "He got me pretty good, too," he added.

My first reaction was annoyance: Didn't my neighbor know it was foolish to approach an aroused dog on his own turf? Why would he ignore Orson's barking, his obvious upset? Why reach a hand over a fence toward a dog that was out of control? Wasn't that asking for trouble?

But I quickly realized that I was being presumptuous, insensitive. Yes, that was not the best way to approach an aroused dog, but could my neighbor really be expected to know that? Why was my first impulse to blame him rather than myself? It wasn't a question of fault—Orson didn't mean any harm, and neither did my neighbor—but a question of facing reality.

My subsequent reactions were more troubling. Neighbors walked up my hill all the time, often with their dogs; children came by to see and feed the donkeys. Elderly people drove by to see the farm, which many had visited in their youth. Technically, my neighbor had behaved foolishly, but others would act similarly. I didn't want them to be bitten, nor did they deserve to be.

Too many dog owners have told me that it wasn't their dogs' fault that some kid got bitten; the child should have been taught to stay away from strange dogs. I don't—can't—agree. If I own a dog like Orson, it's always my responsibility, and in some way my fault, if somebody gets bitten. Legally, perhaps, Orson had not crossed the line. Yet I tended, as many dog lovers do, to dismiss and rationalize. Yes, he nipped—but only at people coming to the gate. He was just doing his job; it's natural for dogs to protect their humans and their territory. Sure, he could be a bit frightening, but only to people who didn't understand dogs.

I even engaged in some of the moral rationalizing that I strenuously object to among other owners: The victim deserved it. He should have known more about dogs, approached the gate more carefully, avoided eye contact, noticed that the dog was excited and backed off.

But that didn't let me off the hook. Orson didn't wake up in the morning and decide whether to be polite that day or not; dogs can't make conscious moral judgments. He reacted instinctively, for reasons I might never fully understand.

But I was wrong to permit any dog to frighten, nip, or bite, then try to explain it away. Every time Orson, or any dog, ferociously charged a gate or nipped a visitor, any time any dog bites a human, the life of every dog suffers. With dog bites an epidemic American health problem—millions of people are bitten every year seriously enough to call the police—I see a particular urgency in making sure my dogs don't hurt anyone.

My first year at Bedlam Farm, we had few incidents, and those that did occur were easy to explain. I lived quietly on my forty-plus snowy acres. Much of that stormy winter even Paula often couldn't make the drive from New Jersey. Delivery people came infrequently. The mailbox was across the road, so the letter carrier didn't have to approach the house. Icebound, focused on writing my next book, I settled into a fairly tranquil routine with my two dogs. We never saw anyone on our walks in the deep woods, and our working and herding lessons took place early in the day, out of others' sight and hearing.

But as the seasons advanced, several developments upset Orson's peaceful equilibrium.

One was the publication of the book we'd been writing

together so cozily, *The Dogs of Bedlam Farm*. People who read about our first year on the farm started visiting uninvited, sometimes bringing their own dogs, sometimes walking up from the village or driving by slowly to take pictures.

Rose ignored most visitors. Sitting by a window or in the yard, watching her sheep, she greeted visitors with a couple of perfunctory woofs. Orson went after each passerby, agitating himself and disrupting our days. Nothing made him crazier than to go outside and see a strange dog down in the pasture, or even in a car across the road. It drove him wild to have people pull up in front of the house to take pictures or stroll around. It made me a bit crazy, too, to have to deal with unexpected visitors, though they were well meaning. Perhaps our reactions were connected.

One morning, as Rose and Orson and I went out for our training session, I discovered a couple and their two German shepherds in the pasture. The dogs were barking at the sheep (at least they were on leashes), and the humans were busy with their cameras. "Oh, we were just passing by," the people said. "Hope you don't mind."

I did mind. The donkeys were eyeing the scene anxiously—to protect the sheep, they would definitely charge or kick at intruders. Rose was about to take off after the two dogs. I managed to grab Orson's collar—he was frantic—before he could do any damage.

The visitors retreated hastily and apologetically. I wanted to be hospitable, and ordinarily would have loved to show off Rose's skills, but these folks were endangering themselves and my animals.

I decided I needed a barrier that would allow the dogs to sit outside and run around safely. There was a dog run out back, but I wanted a fence that enclosed the front yard. It would provide a boundary that visitors and neighbors—and, ultimately, Orson—would respect; it would protect him and them and my privacy.

So Anthony built an elegant white wooden fence, modeled on those you see at horse farms, around the front of the house. It took a while. He had to hand-drill the post holes and measure the boards carefully. He added a layer of green wire mesh so the wily border collies couldn't slip between or under the boards. It took a couple of weeks to construct, but once completed it gave me the freedom to open the front door and simply let the dogs out to take in the sun or have a romp.

I hoped this would offer Orson, and others, protection. My plan was to sit outside with him for a period each day, to make him lie down and stay when a cyclist or hiker or truck passed by, and to shower him with treats when he complied. I would give any owner with a highly arousable dog who loved to run fences the same advice: Use food and calming training to show him, over and over, that visitors are okay. Reinforce and reward him for being calm, instead of yelling and reinforcing him when he barks or chases. Dogs don't really differentiate between good and bad attention; they love either variety.

It was growing apparent that when a truck passed—especially one with a diesel engine—or when a person stood by the gate, Orson would simply lose control. He entered a feverish state in which he would throw himself furiously against the new fence, yapping and growling.

So we undertook more training. At least part of every day was spent waiting for trucks and cars. "Lie down," I would command. After two or three tries, he would, usually. "Stay." Then I tossed treats. Sometimes I sat on the grass next to him, stroking his back, calming him as the hated interloper receded. Sometimes this worked. Sometimes it didn't.

I guiltily reflected that I might have worsened this problem. When Orson (Devon, then) first arrived, he was so out of control that I was desperate to give him something to do, something that would help calm him down and burn up all that energy. The thing I capitalized on was his love of chasing after trucks. I found fenced areas near streets where we could play this game. When a truck came roaring by, I'd say, "Go get 'em!" He loved more than anything to lope after the noise for a hundred yards, then turn back to me. As long as he remained safely behind a fence, it seemed harmless enough.

It's not something I'd recommend now, yet it gave him the chance to run hard, to have work, to feel successful. It never caused aggressive behavior. Now his reactions were more extreme, and I was trying to train him out of the response I used to encourage.

The situation had also changed. It always puzzled me that people would come up to the fence and simply stand there watching while Orson went nuts for ten, even fifteen minutes. They simply didn't know that they were causing, or reinforcing, a problem. But I remained responsible for the behavior of my dog, no matter which side of the fence he was on, even if I had to fight the instinct to lean out the window and beg people to simply go away.

The fence did give Orson a boundary. It was a place I could leave him safely, at least when I was at home, while still giving him and Rose some freedom. I always crated the dogs when I left the farm.

But even with the increase in visitors, this was a rural area. By New Jersey standards, we had scant traffic, few passersby. Apart from the occasional gawker or hapless delivery person who tried to reach over the gate, things were relatively stable for months. Perhaps this would be the pattern of Orson's life—peace alternating with chaos, each new phase an opportunity to work with him, train him, soothe him. Over time, and with patience and persistence on my part, I was sure he would improve.

Built in stages, starting around 1830, my farmhouse is a bit of a hodgepodge. Parts of it are quite elegant, parts in serious disrepair.

The restoration began modestly, as they often do. The latest twist in my ongoing scheme to convince Paula to abandon New Jersey involved renovating an unused bedroom on the second floor to serve as her office. Anthony was doing a spectacular job on it through our second winter, exposing old wooden beams, replacing the drafty windows and cracked walls, refinishing the maple floor.

About Paula: I'd been trying for years to get her to move up to the country, and I was beginning, on one level, to get discouraged, to understand that this probably wouldn't happen anytime soon.

I was luckily and happily married, and one reason was that we had always supported each other's work. Paula entered the workplace when it was an inhospitable place for professional women. Work has never been an abstraction for her but a significant part of her identity and sense of purpose. She'd always been a reporter, from the day I met her in a newsroom, through Emma's early years and beyond. In many ways, Rose reminded me of her—I recognize the risk in comparing your wife to a dog, but those who know Rose and my feelings about her understand this as a compliment—in that work was one of the centerpieces of her life and she would not be happy without it.

Even when we were apart, though, Paula was anchoring. I couldn't have lasted a month without her. She helped financially, oversaw bills and insurance and bank statements, came up whenever she could to help with chores, was deeply involved in my work, especially in reading and editing my first drafts. And because we had both worked for many years as journalists, we were used to frequent absences. We didn't like being apart, but we could handle it.

In recent years, Paula had suffered her own midlife passages. She'd spent a decade and a half as a New York–based reporter for *The Washington Post,* a job she loved. When the paper told her she had to move to Washington—not an option for either of us—she left. But she was very sad to go. She also bore the brunt of our decision to unload our New Jersey home. Almost all the burden of negotiating the sale, shedding decades of possessions, finding an apartment, and moving fell to her. She took it on with her usual tireless efficiency.

Much as she dislikes change, she did well with it. She expanded her teaching at Columbia University, began writing for *The New York Times* and elsewhere, and started work on a book proposal.

Yet she remained a committed urbanite, a New Yorker. Moving to the farm would cut her off from work and make her Mrs. Jon Katz, someone she'd never aspired to be.

She loved having the dogs around, and was happy to take

them for a walk, but was not much drawn to long discussions of their training or emotional lives. She liked visiting the donkeys and distributing carrots, but did not wish to delve into the world of farriers, abscesses, and equine dentistry. She enjoyed walking through Hebron, but would miss indie movies and Thai food and her friends if she moved here for good.

I missed her. Life always felt strange and off-kilter without her.

The good news, though, was that Paula, slowly, was coming to appreciate the farm. She began to build her own life in Bedlam, making her own friends, pursuing her own barn routines (such as feeding the chickens, which she admired for their industrious work ethic), fulfilling a vow made long ago that someday she'd learn to cook. This was a high-priority item in a place where the nearest decent restaurant was at least fifteen miles away.

I was abetting this transition by commissioning her new office. Any place Paula liked had to include her own workspace, and now this one did. Anthony even built her a desk out of beams and lumber found in the barns.

And since he already had to rent a Dumpster to haul out the resulting debris—so went the reasoning—why not pull down the dog room's stained acoustic-tile ceiling at the same time? The unused loft above it could contribute to a soaring space.

The "Dog Room"—as we'd taken to calling it, and still do—was on one end of the house. It looked like a fairly recent addition; I assumed it was an artifact of the early 1960s, with its orange shag carpeting, wood paneling, and fake fireplace.

That carpet had been soiled, clawed, and chewed by cats

and dogs long before mine. It offered so many pungent smells dating back so far that the dogs were happy to claim the room. I put their crates there, and even when they weren't crated, they gravitated to the place and scattered their toys and chewbones on the orange shag. Dogs don't mind old knotty-pine paneling or wonder what's behind an imitation-brick hearth. I did, of course.

On some level, Anthony surely knew the Dog Room would involve more than a new ceiling. I, however, had no clue.

Anthony was, by now, a cross between a friend, a brother, and a son, our evolving relationship limited by our vastly different histories, but increasingly important to us both.

We talked a half-dozen times a day, yelling mock insults, bemoaning some new outrage, sharing our small triumphs. We trekked into Saratoga once in a while for burgers and movies, walked in the woods with our dogs. On Sundays, he and his wife, Holly, and toddler daughter, Ida Jane, and I met for breakfast in Salem.

In the time since I had first seen him patching the sliding door of my newly acquired barn, Anthony and his business had made big strides. He'd originally dubbed his company Hands-On Maintenance and spent his weeks replacing doorknobs and repairing leaky faucets. Now, after he'd tackled increasingly ambitious jobs at Bedlam Farm—from a hillside pole barn for the animals to Paula's airy new quarters—I had some caps made for him that seemed to fit his mission better: *Anthony Armstrong: Repairs and Restorations.* He worked like a fiend, had great taste, and was becoming captain of a small crew of helpers.

Anthony was obsessed with the Dog Room and what might be hidden there. Nobody who lived in or had visited the house had any idea what that fake brick was covering up or why; no one in recent memory had ever looked. There was a decaying chimney on the exterior of the house, and a cast-iron woodstove in front of the fake fireplace, so it seemed safe to assume there'd once been a real fireplace there, or perhaps an oven of some sort.

The plan was for Anthony to tear down the acoustic tile, then insulate and Sheetrock the space above, a start on making the room larger, brighter, less forlorn, more suitable for humans. If we had any money left, we'd pull up that carpet. Insulation was also a priority: when the wind came up hard, the room creaked like an old frigate in a squall and cold air gusted across the floor. I argued, halfheartedly, that the fireplace could wait.

But from the moment he dove in with his crowbar, we both kept looking at that "brick" fireplace. Why was it there? What lay underneath? Anthony couldn't take it. He badgered me for days to let him pry off the wall-covering and take a peek. I'd already spent a hefty sum on the office, plus the winter's usual vet bills and feed. Paula was arguing that Dog Room renovations were a quagmire waiting to happen and could wait.

I'd developed theories about waiting, though. Things I waited to do, I'd learned, often never got done. Few people in life urge you to go for it, to take chances; almost everyone cautions you to be careful, go slow. The trick is to figure out when they're right and when they're wrong. My worst nightmare is a life filled with regrets as the clock winds down. I didn't feel I had as much time to wait as I used to.

So I was already inclined toward adventure, though trying to talk myself out of it, when one April morning Anthony walked past me into the Dog Room with a claw hammer.

"What do you think?" he asked. "Let's poke a hole and take a peek." He knew me well.

He swung his hammer, and it took just three whacks before the "brick" sheared off enough to look behind it. What we saw, when the dust settled enough for a flashlight beam to penetrate, was a complete surprise.

There was a rare old slate fireplace, dusty and crumbling from years of moisture, yet graceful, the sort of discovery renovators dream of. Nearby Granville and environs is a region renowned for its quarries; this rock must have come from there, my neighbors told me as word of the discovery spread. One elderly farmer even thought he remembered the mason who'd built the fireplace.

We saw more sobering things back there, too, alas. Rain had been pouring down the chimney flashing into the walls and floors for years. Nothing much but history was holding the chimney together. There was very little insulation behind the walls, and what was there was water-soaked and smelly.

The rest of the house stood on a stone or concrete foundation, but this room sat right on the ground. So when we proceeded to peel back the carpeting—what the hell—we saw beautiful pine floors that were worn and rotted.

In a bit of a frenzy now, debris and dust beginning to pile up, Anthony ripped off the knotty-pine wall paneling and found more rot and mold.

This was not a recent addition we were seeing but a part of the original house—probably, Anthony thought, a shed used to store firewood for the stoves. "Oh boy, this is going to cost you," he whistled.

When he pulled the ceiling down, the room's history and its destiny became apparent. With its double-height ceiling, rough-hewn old beams, and a barn-wood wall that was once the rear of the house, and with its view of the valley and day-long light, this could be a beautiful space.

"We have to save this room," Anthony and I said, almost in unison. "We have to do it right."

But as I was already learning, the cardinal rule of renovation is that while nobody knows what's behind walls and ceilings, fixing whatever's there or replacing whatever isn't will always take longer and cost far more than you think. Restoring a room, especially one that's nearly two hundred years old, is an organic thing. Everything affects everything else, all the small gears pieces of a greater whole. Anthony immediately hired a helper and bought scaffolding and a bigger truck. I got bigger bills.

Anthony and his sidekick, Chris, were soon going at it, ripping the roof, ceiling, walls, and waterlogged floor apart. Rotted wood, slabs of paneling, tiles and carpeting formed a mountain behind the house. The Dumpster was filled and emptied and filled again. "Oh my God," I heard Anthony say half a dozen times a day as he pulled up another moldy board or poked his crowbar right through a wall.

He hired Kathan, a temporarily out-of-work stonemason, to repoint and rebuild the chimney and restore the fireplace, a task that would take weeks. But Kathan did beautiful work, meticulously remortaring and replacing the crumbling bricks. He was outside on his scaffolding one raw day—I was watching his progress with some awe—when he asked about the gouged-out slope behind the house.

This gaping excavation, an unsightly cutaway dug to make room for cars, trucks, and snowplows to circle the house, was an eyesore. I'd planned to put in a concrete retaining wall to hold back the dirt and prevent mud slides after rain, but hadn't really thought much about the aesthetics. The other option, slightly less unsightly, was to build a wall of pressure-treated lumber.

"You want a stone wall?" Kathan asked.

Genius. Stone walls were beautiful, substantial, dignified. They were everywhere in Washington County, often crumbling in the weeds and woods of former farms, where farmers dug stones from their pastures to make room for crops.

A stone wall would greatly improve Bedlam Farm, and would far outlast me. I loved building things that people might be talking about long after I was gone, like the lovely but slow-growing burr oak I had planted to someday provide shade and beauty in my back pasture. I had no chance of living long enough to see that tree grow tall and spread its branches, but my daughter, Emma, might, or whoever eventually lived here.

So we decided to build the Bedlam Wall, of fieldstone trucked in from a Granville quarry. Had I grasped the expense, noise, and disruption—it took ten tons of stone and a half-dozen truck trips merely to deliver it—I might have hesitated. "On to Berlin," I muttered to Anthony, echoing General Patton.

"If we're gonna go down," he agreed, "let's go down in flames."

Kathan and his helper, Julio, assisted by Anthony and Chris, worked like mules for weeks. The fieldstone—first quarried by workers who fled Ireland during the Potato Famine, we were told—lay piled in giant mounds all over the driveway. Kathan sorted each rock, eyeing it, measuring it, chipping or filing where needed, then fitting it into place. There was no mortar in this wall, just the mason's ability to pile and slide rocks into an interlocking shape. It was extraordinarily complex and painstaking work.

Neighbors and townspeople began stopping by to monitor progress and express admiration. I was buying milk at the Bedlam Corners Variety Store one morning as another customer was gossiping with Marie, its new owner. "That guy is building a huge stone wall up at the old Keyes place. He must be crazy," he said. Then, thinking about it, he added, "He must be loaded, too."

"You're half right," I said, winking at Marie and leaving.

It was hard to believe how these guys worked. They showed up at six a.m., rain or shine, heat or cold, broke for a thirty-minute lunch around noon, then resumed hauling giant rocks around for hours. They manipulated tractors as if they were playing video games. Kathan chiseled and tapped, arranged and rearranged. In the age of The Home Depot, it wasn't something you often got to see.

But it was also a nightmare for Orson.

The din and dust and noise were indescribable and continual. The house rattled with the vibrations of hammers, saws, planers; trucks pulled in and out, dropping bone-jarring loads of rock, followed by the thunk of sledgehammers and the whirs of drills. Neighbors came by in their pickups and muttered about how much money this must cost, how good it looked.

In the midst of it all, I had a book to write. I retreated to my first-floor study while the dust rained down and tried to concentrate. I pulled the dogs in with me, and we all huddled together in my little room.

Rose didn't like the noise, but she found Anthony and his tools the most fascinating thing next to sheep, and would sit and study him for hours from the safe distance of her garden hideaway. Sometimes she would charge at an auger or drill, trying to herd it. Mostly, she decided to become an Anthony scholar, studying him as if he were an ancient text. Clementine also had her work: to enthusiastically greet and lick every human being within her range, and then to gobble every doughnut, sandwich, or cookie she could steal. It was during the Dog Room restoration that I dubbed her The Whore of Bedlam Farm for her willingness to go home with anybody holding a bag of Doritos.

It was sad, in a way, to contrast these two dogs' responses with Orson's.

I had unleashed an Orson hell, an invasion of noisy men with tools, coming in and out of the gate, in and out of the fence and the house, scores of times, day after day, week after week. He fought valiantly to keep them all out, to nip and charge at them, bar the door, grab their tools.

He waited for his moment, took his shots. Anthony's brother, Charlie, having joined the crew to paint, learned to carefully pat Orson and give him treats before entering the yard with sanders and paint cans. Orson seemed to accept him after a few weeks, and Charlie relaxed—until the day he turned away and Orson ran up and nipped him in the butt. Orson does not forget and he does not forgive. And he does not give up.

It all may have taken a toll that I was too busy, self-absorbed, or dim to recognize at first. Orson, as his farm life centered more on me and less on sheep or the outdoors, had become increasingly preoccupied with protecting the boundaries of the house, its gates and doors. Now the coming and going by Anthony and his crew drove him crazy. From dawn to dusk, one large man or another, often carrying a drill, saw, or hammer, was coming through a gate or door to start thumping, banging, noisily intruding.

I crated Orson when I knew people were coming, but I couldn't lock him up all day, and everybody urged me not to.

Anthony and his guys weren't afraid of dogs, and didn't really mind walking into the house holding their toolboxes in front of them, shouting at Orson to get back. They were willing to suffer the occasional ripped pair of jeans. What might have meant a lawsuit in New Jersey was just part of life in the country. Throughout the day, while I worked, I heard people yelling, "Hey, Orson, knock it off!"

In a way, Orson became a bit unhinged. A dog who'd already known too much failure was failing all day, trying to keep out one intruder after another, unable to. In addition to Anthony and his crew, the steady parade of visitors—delivery people, gardeners and mowers, the exterminator, the feed man, neighbors and friends, curious readers—continued.

Some days were worse, some better, but it seemed to me that Orson was being cranked up continuously and danger-ously. I had to try to do something about it, short of sending him to New Jersey for a few months. I went to my vet and told her about my worries.

I told her I wanted to get more serious about this arousal. Might there be a medical cause? We tested and tested. She did blood work, administered a thyroid test, took X-rays. We tested for fractures, for Lyme disease, for cancer. It cost more than a thousand dollars, and turned up nothing.

"I can't help you," the vet finally concluded. "There's nothing medically wrong with Orson that I can see. But I know somebody who perhaps can." She handed me a business card from a holistic orthopedic vet who specialized in dogs with problems that conventional veterinary care couldn't fix.

"She might be a bit out there for you," she cautioned me. "She's a professional and well-trained vet, but she is innovative and open-minded. She does acupuncture and massage and uses herbal remedies. But I can't tell you how many dogs she has helped when I couldn't.

"Orson is a great dog. And I think you're right—something *is* wrong with him. But I can't tell you what it might be. I think your instincts are good. He might be headed for some serious trouble. Valerie may be someone who can help."

I groaned. I didn't want to go there. I liked conventional vets, and was wary of the many "alternative" cures and practices I had seen and heard about, especially online. Surely there had to be rational limits on the amount of time and money I spent worrying about this dog, who was a big part of my life but not all of it.

But my vet was no fuzzy-headed animal wacko. Clear-eyed and businesslike, she'd won my respect and trust. And as a writer about dogs, I thought, I really couldn't lose. It would be interesting either way.

The important measure, I decided, wasn't whether or not I believed in alternative veterinary care, but whether the dog got better. If he did, it was great. If he didn't, wasn't it part of our covenant that I do everything possible to help him, to show him how to live in the world?

Orson, I'd come to fear, was headed for a new kind of trouble. His behavior seemed to be deteriorating in a way I didn't believe ethical or responsible to ignore, not any longer.

He was calmer and more obedient many days, yet on others getting more aroused, his efforts to defend the house more ferocious. We'd been working together for nearly four years. I had trained with him—positively and carefully—over hundreds and hundreds of hours.

I'd run out of ideas, exhausted most conventional training methods, and hit the outer limits of traditional veterinary care.

The number on the card was in Vermont—naturally. I called as soon as I got home. So Orson and I took the next step together and entered the woo-woo.

Orson and Jon

CHAPTER SIX

Hell on Wheels

Orson was never a well-grounded dog. Whatever happened to him back in Texas had left him damaged, without the resilience of dogs like Clem and Rose. He was unraveling, it seemed to me. Among those who knew him, a variety of theories had grown up over the years to try to explain his behavior.

We knew he'd been trained as an obedience show dog at some point, so perhaps that was why gates (like those used in such competitions) had special significance, one breeder suggested.

One vet thought it was perfectly natural for some dogs to defend their territory, but another felt that Orson, when excited, was actually suffering seizure-like symptoms that sometimes caused him to lose control, to fail to recognize even familiar faces and voices. Something like epileptic seizures, she said, that might need to be treated medically, even surgically.

An "animal psychic" I met at a book signing (hers, and there were people lined up beyond the bookstore door waiting to meet her and get their books signed) thought he was picking up distressing vibes from the animals—pigs, chickens and turkeys, cows, a few sheep, too—slaughtered on the farm in years past.

One trainer felt Orson had been poorly socialized as a pup and that I should have visitors bring hamburger and liver treats when they came. Another suggested using a shock collar when he charged the gate.

The odd thing is that Orson, like Clementine, was innately social; he lived for attention. He greeted a steady stream of visitors to the farm warmly and appropriately. He loved the UPS and FedEx men in the driveway—just not when they approached the gate or door. I despaired of ever making sense of these contradictions.

Yet I recognized the truth of what my vet, Mary, was telling me, even as it saddened me. There was no point in subjecting this poked and prodded creature to any more uncomfortable, expensive testing. We had to somehow reach a different kind of accommodation. It was time to move on, if there was anything to move on to.

Holistic. It was an odd-sounding word. The number of dog owners drawn to holistic care kept growing, I knew from my research and from countless stories I'd heard. Yet the idea still discomfited me.

I like and trust regular vets and count a number of them among my friends. I've always found them committed, knowledgeable, and trustworthy. I was doubtful that a holistic vet, whatever that meant, knew much more than regular ones.

I'm also concerned about putting some limits on the care and time I spend on even a beloved dog's well-being. For me, a healthy life with dogs means boundaries. I love my family; I value my work; I treasure my friends—and I love my three dogs dearly. That's about the right order for me. I don't want to spend hours online exchanging herbal cures and trading conspiracy theories about veterinarians and dog-food manufacturers. Holistic care is something I've always resisted as dubious, unnecessary.

Still, Orson and I had kept faith with each other.

And so, two weeks later we drove to a white farmhouse in Manchester, Vermont, where we met Dr. Valerie Gurstein, a vet specializing in holistic care, including acupuncture, chiropractic, and herbal remedies.

Dr. Gurstein's office was different from conventional vets' facilities, which tend to be cramped, crowded, and noisy. Dogs pick up on all sorts of smells and sounds in those situations and often tense up, get fearful or aggressive. "Oh, he knows where he is," people tell me all the time, as even the boldest pets tremble and whine in the vet's waiting room. I have no idea what my dogs think or know, but I see few dogs at ease in such places. Rose gets the shivers the minute we pull into our vets' parking lot, and Orson grows vigilant and anxious. (Clem, the slut, on the other hand, is delighted to be there and wags all the way from the front door to the examining room, happily greeting her many friends and admirers.)

Dr. Gurstein's office was different. We arrived early, but the doctor—soft-spoken and warm—waved us right in. I'd brought Rose along for moral support.

Orson scampered up the porch stairs into the reception area, where something soothing and New Age was wafting from stereo speakers. Dr. Gurstein obviously scheduled visits to avoid tense canine encounters, and allowed plenty of time for each dog, more than an hour. So the atmosphere was altogether relaxed, unhurried.

The examining room felt more like a living room than a medical facility—carpeted, with soft colors and framed art on the walls. The examining table itself was a low carpeted platform less than a foot from the ground. Orson hopped onto it without being asked, showing none of the uneasiness he often demonstrated in conventional veterinary offices.

Dr. Gurstein spoke directly to him in a measured, soothing voice. Trainers often caution that it's unwise to look a dog directly in the eye—many take it as a challenge—but Orson loves people who look squarely at him and say his name; he loves attention in general.

A dog who seems to expect to get into trouble, Orson almost visibly relaxes when he is praised and soothed. He appeared to react to Dr. Gurstein's calm, quiet manner by calming down himself. She let him sniff her hands and check out the room, then sat down next to him on the platform.

"I have to be honest: I'm a bit skeptical about this whole holistic idea," I said. "It's a first for me." She nodded and said she'd heard similar sentiments before. Often, I suspected.

"Before I examine Orson, I'd like to talk to you," she said. "Tell me about your history with him, your experience. I've talked to your vet, but I'd like to know from you why you're here. What do you want for him?"

I was surprised by the question, and more surprised by my response.

My normal vets were great, but decidedly pragmatic. They wanted to identify a problem and fix it, ordering tests as warranted, prescribing medicine when appropriate. They were efficient and highly competent, but the office atmosphere in their busy practice was often chaotic. It was not a place you wanted to linger and schmooze, nor a place where anyone would want you to, since there were always people and patients waiting.

This place was different, and Orson was picking up on it, watching Dr. Gurstein carefully, but at ease, his ears up, his tail wagging, his breathing normal. I was feeling the difference, too. No vet had ever really asked me much about my history with Orson. We usually got right down to symptoms and solutions.

So I told her about how Orson had come to me almost out of the blue, about our difficult first year, about how Orson had led me to sheepherding, which had led me to Bedlam Farm, to donkeys and sheep, and then to Rose and Clementine. I explained what an enormous gift he'd turned out to be. How he'd rescued me from a place I felt estranged from, work I was wearying of, a lifetime without many close friends. How he'd brought me to this life of challenge, beauty, nature, and animals. He had saved me in so many of the ways a person can be saved.

I owed him much, and I felt I needed to take his care and welfare as far as I reasonably could, without offending common sense and perspective. I'd grown very concerned about what could happen if his unpredictable behavior continued. Like it or not—and most of the time I didn't—my farm had become a more public place, with people often streaming through. I had to try harder to calm him.

"A part of him is broken," I said, recounting what little I knew of his early years. "And I can't reach it." My eyes welled up, something that's never happened in all the many times I'd talked about this dog. I'd written reams about Orson; we'd appeared on television and radio; I'd talked about him at readings and lectures—yet I don't think anybody had really asked me how I felt about him, what I wanted for him.

Nor had I really stopped to look back at all the exhausting hours of training, calming, worrying, shouting, soothing, herding, all the work we'd done together. I'd tried so hard to keep faith with this dog, and talking about that with her, the intensity of the experience seemed to seep out. I stopped, took a deep breath, regained control. I didn't particularly like the idea of bawling in a holistic vet's office.

Still, the emotion her question elicited was powerful, and it reminded me just how much I loved this creature, how much he meant to me, how much I wanted to reach and heal that broken part, what was at stake if I couldn't.

The doctor, who suggested I call her Valerie, nodded and listened. Then she spent a long time carefully examining his back, legs, shoulders, and neck for orthopedic problems. Trained as a conventional vet, she was familiar with bone structure and musculoskeletal problems, and quickly found some.

After Orson was hit by that car years ago, he'd rolled to his feet, apparently unhurt, and had shown no damage or injuries when our New Jersey vet checked him over. Nor had the recent battery of tests turned up any orthopedic problems. Now Valerie's exam found extreme sensitivity to being touched along parts of the spine. I could see Orson—the most stoic of dogs—wince sharply, even yelp, when touched in a certain spot.

His spine was seriously out of alignment, she told me; he must be uncomfortable much of the time. That nobody, including me, had noticed this sensitivity in all our time together amazed me. I was suddenly grateful to my vet for suggesting this visit.

I also told Valerie about Orson's arousal problems, how everyday sounds could make him crazy, sometimes even dangerous; how he could switch from placid to furious in seconds, sometimes for no discernible reason. As a demonstration, I clapped my hands. Valerie was startled to see him launch into furious barking, nipping at the air, charging suddenly toward the window, out of control. It was worse around doors and gates and delivery people, I said.

Completing her exam, she suggested Shen calming herbs from China, and recommended acupuncture. I was doubtful about the first idea, bemused by the second. Acupuncture for a dog? That seemed a stretch. Though it had often been suggested for me, for my own bad leg, I always resisted. It seemed somehow fitting that my dog would get acupuncture, but not me. But the measure of this experience, I'd reminded myself, would be simple: Either it helped the dog or it didn't. And we wouldn't know for a while.

Valerie took out a plastic container of acupuncture needles and removed one. Rose, who'd been lying quietly on the floor, watching, suddenly leaped onto the platform over the startled Orson and growled, showing Valerie her teeth. This, too, amazed me: Rose barks at strangers, but has never bared her teeth to anyone. "Easy, Rose," I said sharply.

But I was impressed by the way Valerie handled the confrontation. Instead of trying to placate Rose or scold her, she paused, took one of her needles and held it out for Rose to sniff.

"Rose," she said in that same low, steady voice, "I'm not going to hurt Orson. I'm going to put this needle in him. Watch." Her calm was infectious. She moved the needle to Orson, who was lying peaceably on his side, watching, then back to Rose so she could sniff it again, then back to Orson. Rose, whose studious, problem-solving nature has mesmerized me more than once, followed the needle with her eyes, head tilted. Valerie waited a few seconds while Rose considered.

Rose seemed satisfied by this and hopped off the table and resettled herself on the floor, watchful but willing to let things proceed.

That first day, Valerie inserted eight or nine needles into Orson's back, neck, and shoulders. At first he tensed. Then, needle by needle, he seemed to steadily relax.

I was stunned, after ten minutes or so, to see him lying on his side, sound asleep, snoring loudly, his tongue hanging from one side of his mouth while needles protruded from various parts of him. My dog, usually so intense, anxious, and alert, was barely conscious, practically comatose.

At the end of the session, Valerie removed the needles and turned to a cabinet stocked with treats. Orson came to, but was as relaxed as I could remember ever seeing him outside my own office. After the first visit, Orson learned to step off the platform and sit by the cabinet.

We came every two or three weeks for a chiropractic adjustment and acupuncture; in between, I administered calming herbs, mixing a teaspoonful or so into his food each day.

Orson seemed eager for his treatment. When we arrived

at Valerie's office, he dashed out of the truck to her door, ran inside, and jumped onto the examining table, usually lying down before he was asked. At times, the needles made him uncomfortable and he squirmed. Valerie, seeing things I never could, adjusted the needles until he slowly closed his eyes, sighed deeply, and conked out.

Usually Orson is a pain when we drive, rushing from one window to the other as cars and trucks whiz by. But when we left Valerie's, he went out like a light and slept all the way home.

Almost everybody who knew this dog—especially the guys still working on the wall and Dog Room—volunteered that Orson had changed, that he seemed easier, less frantic. He still got excited at the gate, and still took the occasional nip at somebody carrying a power tool, but it seemed an almost half hearted gesture.

"Knock it off, Orson," Chris or Anthony or Kathan would say, and he would. Sometimes when somebody came to the door, he didn't even get up—this from a dog who once crashed through a Plexiglas-braced leaded-glass window.

I judged that he was about 30 percent calmer, 90 percent of the time, the most dramatic behavioral change I had witnessed in the last few years.

If the gauge of holistic care was whether or not the dog did better, my first encounter with alternative medicine was a success. I was happy that I'd tried it. Clearly there's a point where conventional veterinary care—as good as it is, as happy as I've been with it—has nothing much to offer and another realm of medicine begins.

Still, I was unprepared when Valerie, after several months, suggested I speak with an animal communicator. "I'm not ready for that," I protested.

Acupuncture? Some herbs? A dose of Enya, followed by some sweet talk, a soothing massage, and some hypoallergenic treats? So far, so good—but no farther.

Valerie said she understood.

But she didn't give up. A couple of weeks later, Valerie suggested I give her a picture of Orson to pass along to a shamanic soul retriever, a woman who'd studied the ancient Chinese notion that when animals are damaged, parts of their souls break off and can, under certain circumstances, be retrieved and returned to them. This retriever had a solid reputation for helping animals; Valerie recommended her enthusiastically. She'd intended to return to the subject of an animal communicator, but was waiting until she sensed my "resistance" had lowered.

My discomfort, in fact, remained high; this seemed a trek deeper into la-la land. But I agreed to think about it. If I were seriously exploring alternative care for Orson, shouldn't I go all the way? The point of any potential treatment isn't whether I "believed" in it. If Orson got better, then it worked—at least for him. If he didn't, it didn't.

Pieces of soul break off from a dog when he or she suffers? I just can't put together how that would work. But I'd also observed how conventional training and veterinary medicine weren't working for him, either.

On top of that, a friend in Vermont called to say that a well-known horse communicator—someone with decades of experience around racetracks and horse breeders, with many stellar references—was branching out into dogs and other animals. She wanted to come to the farm and see Orson and the donkeys. She was also, my friend added, picking up signals from Winston, the differently abled rooster.

Well, I told Paula, the same test applies. If the dog got better, it was worth the shot. In for a dime, in for a dollar.

Lesley, the shamanic healer, called first. All she needed to begin with was a picture of the dog, she said. She might or might not need to visit the farm and see Orson after that. She didn't even mention payment until I did. When I pressed her, she said she charged very little—thirty-five dollars for the "retrieval," another thirty or so if a visit was necessary. Obviously, she wasn't driven by money.

Then Donna, the horse communicator, e-mailed me from Virginia. She seemed bright and direct, and a lot more expensive: $400 to communicate with Orson, Rose, and Clementine, plus the three donkeys. She'd throw in the rooster for free.

Donna pulled into the driveway in her SUV a couple of weeks later. Tall, blond, and lean, she had the look of a horse person, that ruddy complexion, that confidence around animals. She'd been doing this for twenty years, she told me, shaking hands firmly, and then following me out to the yard. There seemed nothing woo-woo about her.

She stood over Orson and waved one hand over his back. "He's telling me he's frightened," she announced. "He thinks you might give him away, like you did the other dog"—evidently a reference to Homer, now resettled with my neighbor back in New Jersey.

She walked around a bit with Orson, and then told me that Orson was a border collie in need of a job. "He is confused. He wants to work, and you *are* his work. He is very upset at all the people coming here. He wants to protect you, and he thinks that he's failing whenever somebody comes in."

I didn't say much as she visited with the other dogs. Clementine kept bringing her bones and treats; I could hardly wait to hear what was going on inside *that* head. "Clementine is upset when Rose gets on the couch and takes her spot," she said, picking up nothing further. It made sense that this sweet and uncomplicated creature had no bigger complaints.

Out by the barn, Donna met Winston, who was, she said, one "irritated" bird, the Rodney Dangerfield of roosters. He got no respect. Rose was always plowing over him to reach the sheep, Clementine would steal the chicken feed from under his beak.

"Has a hen died or left?" Donna asked. Yes, I said, I'd returned one to the friend who'd given her to me; I didn't need so many eggs.

"Well, next time tell Winston," she advised. "He is looking for her and is distressed that he can't find her." *Tell him?* I wondered. Did we speak the same language?

I appreciated Donna's perceptive readings; she picked up on some important stuff. I'd long known that one of Orson's elemental dramas was that he was a border collie without work. That I had become his work was likely true, and many people would find it touching, but I was more ambivalent. Hanging out with a human isn't the natural task of a border collie. Her perceptions of Orson were useful and reinforcing to hear. And while I didn't particularly care if I'd annoyed Winston, who had quite a nice rooster life, Donna did know and understand animals, I concluded.

At the same time, hers were ideas that plenty of good

trainers or behaviorists—or farmers, for that matter—might have come up with. I was fuzzy about the difference between what was observed and what was "communicated."

And I found it off-putting when Donna paused, closed her eyes, and received supposed messages from the dogs: "Orson is telling me his shoulder hurts." Was she receiving literal words, in English, from these animals, I asked her more than once, or just relaying her sense of their thoughts?

"Oh, they're talking to me," she said. "These are their literal words." Sometimes she laughed at their "jokes." With that she lost me.

I debated this visit with friends for months afterward. Probably it's healthy and valuable to explore alternative ways of communicating with our animals. But I found it arrogant to assume that animals would use our words. Their animalness is practically sacred to me, and I respect and love them for it. Interpreting behavior is one thing; picking up verbal jokes quite another, a place I couldn't go.

So I was especially wary when Lesley Nase, the shaman, called to say she was receiving "fascinating images" from Orson, from the picture I'd given Valerie. She would love to come to the farm and see him, she suggested, and explore whether there were places he might be getting "negative energy."

Lord, I thought. In a country where millions of people don't have basic health care, my border collie is getting visits from communicators and shamans. But I had gone this far.

Lesley showed up the following week in a tiny foreign car, a middle-aged woman clutching a handful of dowsing rods. I liked Lesley, too; she was warm and funny, joking about retrieving souls. I was struck by how the dogs—especially Orson—warmed to her.

She also pointed out the irony, noticing my limp, of Orson's getting regular acupuncture while I didn't. Did I want some energy treatment for my leg, she wondered. No thanks, I said.

I think by now Orson had figured out when someone was coming to care for him. He'd always craved being the center of attention, elbowing other dogs aside to greet visitors, curling up in almost anybody's lap. So he was shortly in Lesley's, as we all sat in a heap on the front porch steps. He's too large and heavy to really be a lap dog, but she didn't seem to mind.

"I got an image of a Nazi parade from Orson" was her opening revelation. "He was inside gates and fences, and there were people marching, and other people watching and clapping."

Orson had once been an obedience show dog, I told her; he'd often entered competitions through fences and gates, although I'd never been sure how that connected to his arousal and nipping. A woman who'd known Orson back in Texas had e-mailed me after a previous book to say that some competitors on the circuit there were referred to as "Nazi obedience trainers," because they were so critical of their dogs. As in any sport, from human soccer games to canine herding trials, people do get swept up in the passion of competition, which can become something ugly, an arena for enforcing control rather than working together.

The "images" Lesley was receiving—somehow—made me picture some of the worst herding and obedience competitions I'd attended. I could picture Orson in a show ring, entering and leaving through gates, aroused by the applause, growing frenzied—and then distracted. He hated almost all direct commands, even from me. Before he got his new name, he cowered, winced, and panted—almost every avoidant behavior a dog can show when confronted with something fearful or strange.

A Nazi parade. It gave me a bit of a jolt.

I appreciated that Lesley wasn't claiming to hear Orson's voice, but rather felt she was picking up images that helped explain him. Behaviorists argue that dogs don't have language and cannot think in human terms. Some behaviorists believe that dogs' thoughts consist of sensory ideas, which take the place of words. Other scientists use phrases like "movies of the mind" when they try to interpret dogs' mental abilities; images drawn from experience substitute for words in their canine heads.

There's a long, rich history of humans who have special gifts that enable them to understand and receive information from animals. This therapeutic communication with the spirit world often comes through dreams or visions, even hallucinations, during which animal spirits explain the sources of their problems and provide guidance for finding a cure.

Certain individuals are believed to possess such unusual visionary powers that they can enter the spirit world at will. For thousands of years, these people have been known as shamans. They're credited with having an unusual affinity with the spirits of animals. I'd heard of such people and read about them.

Lesley might have been one of them. If you accept the concept of dogs thinking in sensory images—movies of the mind—and that some people might have unusual receptivity to such images, then her work didn't seem so outlandish.

For whatever reason, I felt she'd read Orson accurately and grasped the complex nature of our relationship.

Like many dog lovers, I am extraordinarily attuned to my three. I usually know if they're in pain, aroused, fearful, or uneasy. I often anticipate their behaviors—from upchucking to barking—as they do mine. I've had a number of dreams about Orson, no doubt linked to difficult parts of my own past, as well as to the animal parts of myself. On occasions, when I'm with him, images of fear and pain have flashed through my mind quickly, a kind of waking vision.

So perhaps Lesley just took these instincts further, somehow. Since I didn't really believe I could literally read Orson's or my other dogs' minds, I'd never really tried. But I kept in mind my midlife motto: Learn and grow.

I didn't quite grasp the notion of soul retrieval, or how Lesley's dowsing around the grounds could help matters. But what I believed was less important than what helped the dog. This whole excursion into strange new territory wasn't about me, but him.

Lesley had good, solid ideas about helping Orson: keeping him with me more when I wrote, keeping him out of the yard when I wasn't there, sprinkling the gates with food and beef jerky each morning so that, over time, he would come to see them as less dangerous. Equally important, she reminded me to make certain he was given the opportunity to succeed and be praised, for his battered canine ego to be strengthened, even rebuilt. Her counsel was both apt and utilitarian, something I could translate into practical action.

She felt a positive connection with me, she said, and felt she had a good grip on the dog. A bit to my surprise, I wanted to stay in touch with her. Of my dogs, Lesley said, only Orson had broken pieces of his soul floating around out there. At least, only Orson was damaged to the extent that she received powerful imagery from him. Which was interesting, because he was the only dog I hadn't raised from puppyhood.

So we agreed to talk by phone in a few weeks, to see what else she might glean.

By this point I felt as if I were living in a movie, a story full of ghosts and spirits, dim flashbacks and unearthed secrets.

The script called for me to accept the communicators and shamans and move, along with my dog, to a higher level of consciousness. Some friends were delighted, praising my open-mindedness; others clearly thought I'd lost my marbles.

What Orson needed was to be treated appropriately for his physical ailments and to be trained—still more—for his behavioral problems. Anything else was just letting myself off too easy.

But how tempting. How I wished he *could* talk to me, tell me what had happened to him, why he felt so anxious and unsafe, how I could help. What wouldn't I pay for the glue that would put his broken parts back together, and give him contentment for his remaining years? He had done so much for me, I would be happy to return the favor. If Orson had taught me anything, it was that he isn't like me, doesn't reason like me, and, sadly, can't talk to me. He was an instinctive and wounded animal, not a four-legged human waiting for a therapist—or spiritual advisor—to tap into his childhood.

Ultimately, though, what these communicators told me, regardless of how they received the information, was something I already knew but needed to hear again and again: I had more work to do with this dog.

It would be interesting to have a personal shaman, I told Orson. "When you've got problems, send signals to her," I advised him. "Don't nip at people."

As it happened, relief for Orson was definitely on the way,

but it didn't come from the land of extrasensory perception. The thing that brought Orson the most delight that year was an expensive gadget, a farm implement, something with an internal-combustion engine.

Several weeks after Lesley's visit, John Sweenor—mechanic, friend, neighbor, a member of our strange and growing little tribe at Bedlam—came by and saw me hobbling. I'd had a bad left ankle for years, and wore orthotics and a leg brace to keep from falling. Sometimes, walking as much as I did around the farm was painful.

By that spring, however, I'd developed worsening, almost blinding pain in my right leg—the supposedly good one. The diagnosis was a torn quadricep, probably caused by climbing the steep hills around the farm, hauling lambs and supplies up and down the slopes. The pain was relentless, exhausting, dispiriting.

The injury would take weeks to heal, the doctor said, and would heal only if I stayed off those hills and off my leg. This was both difficult and uncomfortable. I loved walking; the dogs and I strolled for hours around the farm and through the adjacent woods. And I loved sheepherding, which also involved a lot of movement. Even a quiet visit with donkeys required making my way up a steep incline.

Anthony and John had been badgering me ever since I arrived to buy an ATV, an all-terrain vehicle—or four-wheeler, as they're called upstate. ATVs are somewhat controversial. Teenagers or irresponsible drivers can steer them into grisly accidents. And environmentalists hate the idea of noisy machines penetrating quiet wooded places, burning fossil fuel and spewing fumes.

I hated the idea for different reasons: ATVs offended my middle-aged ego. "They're like golf carts," I sniffed. "I don't need a machine to get around my own farm." Increasingly, though, I did. If I didn't rest my now bad leg, I wouldn't recover. If I couldn't recover, how could I maintain this wonderful, but physically demanding, life in this lovely place?

One day John drove up with his own ATV on a trailer and rolled it out for me to test-drive. It was fun maneuvering the thing down the wooded paths and around the rolling meadow. And it was a pleasure to climb up into the pasture without hurting. But I already had a farm truck and an SUV and didn't relish calling Paula to suggest buying still another vehicle.

John and Anthony both argued that I needed one. ATVs were useful, they said, good for hauling hay and firewood and trash. It was also fun to go trekking to nearby farms or into the woods. One thing I'd noticed—and often argued with environmentalist friends about—was that people like Anthony don't use such contraptions to despoil nature but to experience it. He and his friends are constantly out in fields and woods on four-wheelers and snowmobiles; he tosses his daughter, Ida, into her seat and heads out for picnics and river explorations.

"I don't think I can buy one right now," I protested to John. But my heart was sinking. Doctors can say what they want, but there was no way to maintain a farm with three dogs, three donkeys, three chickens, and a lot of ewes in labor while staying off one's feet.

So a few days later, I went to the dealer with John and, as both he and Anthony knew I would, returned with a Kawasaki Prairie. John gave me a long lesson on operating it safely; Anthony showed me how to climb steep hills and make turns.

Then I was alone with it, a snappy dark-green model with wide, steady tires. The machine was almost shockingly simple to use: You turned the key, adjusted the choke, and then drove off, using a throttle near your right thumb. John had insisted I buy a helmet; he also installed a rear seat, in case Paula, Emma, or a dog needed a ride.

The dogs gathered around the ATV curiously. I couldn't envision a dog riding in that seat, but I was wrong. Orson hopped up and planted himself in it as if he'd been born there, waiting for me to take him four-wheeling, apparently. So I climbed on, trying to spare my painful leg. He put his head over my right shoulder, to navigate, and off we puttered, slowly, down a path into the woods.

Omigod, I remember thinking as we launched, the wind in my face, Orson's head on my shoulder. *I've wasted my life.*

Orson was completely at ease. With his tremendous agility, he kept his footing over every bump and turn. I accelerated a bit and we zipped around the meadow. When I pulled back into the driveway, having kept our first excursion brief, Orson waited until he was sure I wouldn't change my mind and crank the thing up again. Then he leaped down, looking delighted with himself.

The dogs instantly loved this new contraption. They loved the running, and the sense of adventure. Rose, who wanted no part of riding, was happy to take up point position about a dozen yards ahead. She never had to break a trot to keep well ahead of me, no matter how fast I went. Clementine, surprisingly fleet for a Lab, trotted right alongside or to the rear. Orson sometimes ran but usually rode.

We found new streams and trails in the woods, stopped for picnics. I started packing sandwiches and treats, plus water for us all. The border collies never tired of running alongside, but after a few miles, Clem did, so I sometimes lifted her onto the seat.

Orson had a shaman and two vets, one holistic and one traditional. He had been studied by behaviorists and trainers. His diet included Chinese herbal supplements. I'd trained him year after year. I've read countless books, tried innumerable treats, methods, and programs, talked to vets, behaviorists, herders.

I can honestly say that none of those efforts changed this strange dog as dramatically as my ATV. The Helldog, as he was known in my family, became: Hell on Wheels. The ATV somehow meshed happily with his crazy self.

He had found his work—intense, exciting, in close proximity to me. Unlike sheepherding, which he had to watch from a distance, on the ATV he was in the center of the storm, right where he always wanted to be. The machine gave him the chance to run like a fiend, which he loved, and then to navigate, which he loved even more. And there was no way to do it wrong or screw it up. It was all positive, all the time.

Every morning when I came outside, he took up position on the rear seat, awaiting travel instructions. If we were doing something else, he jumped down and followed along. If we were ATV-ing, he was in heaven. He'd never loved working with sheep nearly so much. The border collie who needed work had found some, and it calmed him even more than Chinese herbs.

Over the past months, Rose had pushed Orson aside a bit. She'd gained importance because she was so indispensable, and because dealing with the sheep was so big a part of farm life. Clem was irresistible to everyone; people lined up to see and cuddle with her. But this machine provided Orson's triumphal comeback. I didn't really know how it related to whatever had been bothering him. But I know he was a different dog, less frenetic, more at ease.

The ATV had other purposes. It would give my leg a chance to begin healing. The wagon that attached to the rear *was* useful; I used it to haul manure for the gardens, bales of hay, firewood for the stoves. Aboard the ATV, I drove up to the top of the pasture each morning and night to check on the ewes and lambs, visit the donkeys, and monitor fences that can't be seen from the house. I surprised coyotes, rescued a ewe stuck in a thorn bush. But the machine's greatest contribution was harder to quantify or describe.

One early summer morning, I left Rose and Clem in the yard. Orson hopped up onto the ATV and we roared off. I had packed my lunch and a marrow bone for him. At the top of the pasture, we motored over to the brown Adirondack chairs, with their thrilling view. In the past, I'd clambered up there almost daily, but since my other leg started hurting I rarely used those chairs.

At the top of the hill, I took in the lovely breeze, unpacked my sandwich, and gave Orson his bone to gnaw on. We watched the puffy clouds move slowly over the fields, listened to crickets and cicadas. After a while, Orson put his head on my foot and napped. I had a strong feeling I rarely got from this difficult creature: peace. It was nice.

In June, I decided Orson and I were ready to take our act on the road. I checked the firmness of the belts holding the backseat in place, and waved Orson aboard. We headed down the dirt road and into town, right down the middle of Route 30.

Strictly speaking, this was not legal. But it sure was fun. A rottweiler roared out of a yard and gave chase. In any other context, there would have been a brawl, a drama, with barking, charging dogs, and anxious humans. But this time, Orson looked down at this dog with contempt and just blew him off. Orson barked once or twice; I yelled insults; we cruised on.

We drove by Mrs. O'Malley sitting in her garden and watched her jaw drop. We zipped past the Presbyterian church and waved at the Reverend Hoffman. We saw Don Coldwell in his workshop, crafting more Adirondack chairs.

When we pulled up to the Bedlam Corners Variety Store, Marie came out and gave me a soda. "How did you get here?" she asked, incredulously, staring at Orson, who seemed to relish his role as grand marshal of his own parade. ATVs are not supposed to go cruising down highways.

Next, keeping to the side of the road, we headed for Gardenworks, the sprawling garden and farm center at the edge of town. As we roared up to the front door, its owner, Meg Southerland, blinked and smiled. Orson hopped off for some water, which his fans among the staff were happy to provide, and I proudly showed off my new vehicle. Everyone looked around for the trailer that had transported it from the farm, but of course there wasn't one.

"You didn't," said Meg, who'd grown used to my odd adventures but was nonetheless alarmed.

"I did."

After a few minutes spent visiting, though, it was time to head home. I didn't want to press my luck and run into a sheriff's deputy or state trooper.

But we were almost alone on the road, it turned out, chugging back down Route 30, past the variety store and the church, past Mrs. O'Malley and the rottweiler, and up the hill to the farm, where Clem and Rose were in the yard, waiting to greet us.

How strange a sight we must have been, man and dog. All we needed were silk scarves to look like flying aces, like Snoopy and the Red Baron.

It was a victory march. Orson could not have been happier, prouder, more at ease. Perhaps we both sensed it was some kind of high-water mark, after all our hard work, training, needles, tests, and herbs. I have never loved him more than at that moment.

If parts of Orson's soul remained scattered, maybe we'd picked up one or two on our procession. I'd have to check with his personal shaman. Meanwhile, we were a happy duo.

CHAPTER SEVEN

Ecstatic Places

I hadn't thought about my fish for years. It was Paula who reminded me of my aquatic companions. They were the dogs of my childhood.

I was obsessed with tropical fish—betas, mollies, guppies, tetras—between the ages of eight and twelve, the first of several great obsessions. At first, no one outside of my family knew of their existence, and no one inside my family cared.

I launched this enterprise at the J. J. Newberry five-and-dime store in downtown Providence, where a bald and businesslike one-armed man, who always wore a white shirt and tie, ran the fish department. A blunt sort, he never asked a single question about me, not even my name. But he was generous in telling me all he knew about fish, which was a great deal.

Before long, I had six or seven tanks—at least four of

them held twenty-five gallons—hooked up to an elaborate system of thermostatic heaters, lights, gurgling pumps. Fish, tanks, and related equipment took over my room and much of the upstairs.

All these elements I laboriously hauled through busy streets and transported on buses and up long blocks to our aging, sprawling house miles away. It took months, even years, to fully assemble this world. To pay for it all, I regularly stole money from my mother's purse. I don't know to this day if she noticed and said nothing, or didn't notice, or didn't want to.

Over time, I learned to breed fish to sell and trade, supervising matings and innumerable hatchings. I was the house physician, as well, performing surgery and removing sores and tumors. I constructed elaborate surgical netting with lights to trap sick fish and hold them while I worked. I saved many fish lives, and lost some others.

I ordered medicines from different parts of the country so I could treat funguses and bacterial infections. After a while, strangers began to call and ask me to come save their fish, and I would grab my bag of surgical instruments, lamps, and medicines and wait to be picked up.

My parents had no idea where I was going, or when I would be back. They thought my passion for fish strange, anyway. My father believed young boys should be playing baseball, and my mother never once set foot in my fish room, to my knowledge. They were in their own worlds; the fish were mine.

My companion in this private realm was Sam, my willful basset hound, a dog from another era. Nobody ever trained him or cleaned up after him; he was never walked on a leash. In the morning, rain or shine, someone let him out the back door; in the afternoon, someone let him back in. In between, he hung around the yard, eating garbage and dozing.

Inside, he was so insistent on sleeping in my narrow little bed that he often shoved me right out onto the floor, then growled or nipped if I tried to climb back in.

Whenever I wasn't in school, I was up in my room with Sam and my fish. The lights above the tanks hummed and reflected off the colored gravel; the whole room had an eerie, underwater sort of glow. Lying in bed at night, I stared for hours at the rhythmic swimming, circling, and eating that marked the lives of fish.

Each tank had its own design, its own little concrete and plaster community, complete with houses and castles, pirate ships and treasure chests. I'd constructed elaborate ecosystems with fake coral reefs and real plants. Windmills turned, tiny divers raised and lowered their arms, dragons blew bubbles from their noses. Periodically I undertook massive cleanups, involving the transfer of fish, the draining of tanks, the scraping of glass and boiling of gravel. The pumps and filters needed constant maintenance. I liked knowing I could always reassemble everything afterward.

Up in my room, my little kingdom grew. No caustic teachers, nasty kids, troubled siblings, quarreling parents. Fish lives are simple, revolving around one another and food.

I saw the one-armed man two or three times a week, and he proved a ready and lucrative market for the scores of baby fish I was cranking out in my bedroom. And I needed constant infusions of cash. Riding public transit buses, clutching unstable plastic bags filled with fish—this method of transport had a high casualty rate.

Life in my room wasn't simple, either. Lightbulbs blew out, filters filled with gunk, equipment malfunctioned. The floor was piled with fish magazines full of counsel about filtration systems, gravel, and food. Since fish do not live long, they had to be continually replaced. It was common to come home from school and find dead fish floating; I flushed them unceremoniously down the toilet.

My toughest, and most lucrative, work was breeding Siamese fighting fish, those vivid fantailed fish, usually kept in tiny bowls, that puff up colorfully at the sight of one another. (I was also proud of having crossbred mollies with platys, something rarely achieved by amateurs.)

Breeding the fighting fish—betas, they are properly called—is a laborious process. The male blows a bubble nest at the top of the tank, then fertilizes the eggs his mate lays and places each egg in a bubble. The parents have to be separated promptly before he can harm her, but separated without disturbing the fragile nest of bubbles, subject to disintegration at the slightest disturbance.

It was a painstaking process for all involved, but the one-armed man paid top dollar for the babies. After a while, I didn't have to steal money for fish or equipment.

As I monitored my pregnant fish, separating the newborns from predators, Sam lay at my feet for hours. I appreciated his companionship. I thought him immensely loyal—no one else ever wanted to enter this water world—but perhaps he had his own agenda. (When we moved to southern New Jersey a few years later, so that my father could take a new job, my parents gave Sam away. It seemed ridiculous to them, not even worth discussing, to move two hundred miles with a dog.)

One night our family was having dinner downstairs when

I heard what sounded like a series of thumps, followed by tin-kling glass. My mother was the first to notice water dripping from the chandelier over the table—my bedroom was just above the dining room—and onto our dinner plates. She screamed.

I ran upstairs as quickly as I could. The central monitor that controlled all the heating units for the tanks had short-circuited and blown out the sides of every tank. The mess was astounding—water, gravel, plants, broken glass, and flopping fish all over the floor.

Sam was rushing from one corner of the room to another, gulping down as many of my fish as he could. Afterward, he threw up for days. We were picking out dried-up carcasses from behind radiators and dressers for weeks.

When I came across environmental psychologist Louise Chawla's mesmerizing article "Ecstatic Places," it was as if I'd come across a key to understanding my own life.

Chawla, who writes about childhood, nature, and creativ-ity, went back to the ancient Greek for the original meaning of *ecstatic*. Most of us use the word to describe delight or joy. But the word's root sense (*ek* + *stasis*) has to do with "stand-ing apart," or "standing outside ourselves," and Chawla uses it to describe an intense memory or experience that affects a child who goes on to become a creative adult.

Such memories vary, but often they involve simple affec-tion for a place where one has felt "comfortable, secure and well-loved," a place that often—though not always—in-cluded nature and seemed "imbued with life."

Chawla's notion is that such environments offer a child freedom, a sense of enormous potential, an openness to discovery. These places "beckoned enthrallingly." And they can be transforming. "We do not need to consciously preserve these memories; we know that we can never lose them," Chawla writes. "They are like radioactive jewels buried within us, emitting energy across the years of our lives."

She sees a deep, though still poorly understood, link between nature and creativity. Ecstatic memories, Chawla suggests, provide us with "meaningful images; an internalized core of calm, a sense of integration with nature, and for some, a creative disposition."

If disconnection from nature is a form of social suicide, and triggers alienation and loneliness, as some psychoanalysts argue, then experiences in nature when we are young can shape our imaginations and affect our lives forever after.

I now live in an ecstatic place, one that daily takes me outside myself and into nature. Ecstatic moments have become an integral part of life here, as commonplace as encounters with plumbers or cranky customer-service reps.

The histories of people who create things for a living— books, buildings, paintings, woodwork—often include stories of how the imagination is sparked and nourished by glancing occurrences that only in retrospect appear significant—encounters with flowers in bloom, city lights at night, birds in a nest. These memories and experiences become embedded in the imagination, and echo through our lives.

Ecstatic places can also be interior or urban. What they have in common, Chawla says, in addition to an association with the physical freedom of discovery, is the psychological freedom of undisturbed encounter. They occur beyond the pale of friends, outside the direction of parents and teachers.

Alone, free from intrusion, distraction, surveillance, and prohibition, the child is free to encounter a place spontaneously. The place, in a sense, belongs to the child; he's not an interloper in someone else's territory, but feels the place is his own.

I got chills coming across these ideas in someone else's book. Lights began switching on in my head about me, my farm, my ecstatic encounters, my freedom from intrusion, distraction, surveillance, and prohibition.

If any single notion defined my own early life, it would be undisturbed encounter. I drifted from place to place, alone and unobserved. It remains my most comfortable state.

So much memory of my early life has dissipated, whole years blurred or vanished, that it seems to me my life began when I married Paula and we had our daughter, Emma. I am a lucky and often happy man, my life filling with riches. That my childhood was very different is a testament to the fact that one part of life need not inevitably determine the outcome of the rest.

Growing up in Providence, with few friends or interests outside my fish and comic books, I drifted through empty days, often skipping school, wandering.

I felt as close to rocker Buddy Holly as anybody. My "friends" were bus drivers, retail clerks, and waitresses in the places I visited regularly—like Dolly, the counter waitress at the Sheraton Hotel downtown, who gave me pieces of pie, and the one-armed czar of tropical fish at Newberry's.

Before and (especially) after the destruction of my fish universe, I haunted the city, walking for hours, riding buses and trolleys, visiting pet stores downtown, eating dinner at hot dog stands, knowing where to seek shelter from rain or cold. I bought coins, cards, trinkets, and books, usually with stolen money. I snuck into old movie theaters and befriended street vendors.

Since I hated school, but rarely wanted to go home afterward, either, especially once my fish were gone, Sam and I developed a new headquarters in one of the family vaults in a vast, unkempt, and little-traveled cemetery on North Main Street, a half mile from our home.

The vault sometimes seemed fearful, but mostly tranquil. Well away from the street, reached via shady paths, it was dark and dank, perhaps ten or twelve feet high and twice as long, constructed of a thick stone, now gritty, worn, and water-stained. On sunny days, light streamed in through a couple of skylights; on cloudy days, it was very dark. And even in the middle of summer the enclosure was chilly.

Inside lay several generations of Sandersons, their names chiseled into the stone. Sam and I encamped in front of Nicholas's resting place. I can't remember when Nicholas Sanderson was born, but the year of his death is etched in my mind: 1942. I often imagined him a war hero, killed in combat. He was, I was sure, a pilot who went down bravely after a fiery battle in the clouds.

The vault wasn't a gloomy place; it was my place. I ate candy bars and peanut butter crackers and daydreamed there. Sam generally curled up in a corner of the vault to sleep, his snores often echoing in the chamber.

I was careful to clean up my wrappers and leave no trace of my presence. Once or twice the police spotted Sam and me on the way in or out of the cemetery and drove us both home, with appropriate scolding and lectures. They thought we might be vandals; at times, they feared we might also become victims. They and my parents warned me to stay away.

But we caused no damage, and after a while, we were almost always able to avoid being spotted. The police don't like to wander around cemeteries any more than most people.

Nobody else ever came into the vaults, just as nobody seemed to notice a kid hanging around a quaint old downtown in the middle of a weekday. So I could continue taking refuge in the vault. It was there I cried for Buddy Holly when his death in a plane crash was announced on the radio, there I constructed a life for Nicholas Sanderson and fed Sam bits of hot dog and bread.

As we grow older, we selectively recall those memories, incidents, and images we believe significant. The thread of my own life, my own story, it suddenly seemed to me, provided a straight line from Sam in the cemetery to Orson and the farm. Both dogs had accompanied me or led me to ecstatic experience, shaped who I was or wanted to be.

In my water world, I did experience the freedom Chawla talks about, a sense of potentiality, an openness to exploration and discovery in a place that was unquestionably enthralling. Later, my stone hideaway among the dead, and the streets and stores of old downtown Providence, served much the same purpose.

I would have said I had an uneasy relationship with nature, which I always saw as the province of environmental do-gooders and sappy documentaries. I was sent to a summer camp when I was a kid, wet my cot most nights, got eaten alive by bugs, was terrified of the water, and hated every second of outdoor life. For decades, I didn't feel drawn to return.

I don't like heat, dirt, things that crawl or fly through the woods at night. I've never understood the charm of camping, sleeping on hard ground, battling mosquitoes. I became a committed city dweller, living most of my life in places like

Boston, Philadelphia, Washington, Baltimore, and Dallas. When we weren't working, Paula and I happily haunted restaurants, theaters, galleries, and bookstores.

But caring for fish, creating my own world for them, learning how to breed and heal them, *was* involvement with nature, even though almost everyone who knew me thought me a strange, withdrawn, sedentary child. Like dogs, fish don't leave or say cruel things or lose their tempers. They allowed me to provide soothing, nurturing, and safe environments for them. In doing so, I created my own sanctuary, and if I wasn't always happy there, the experience almost perfectly reflects the idea of the ecstatic place.

The destruction of my collected aquaria and inhabitants may seem a sad conclusion to the story, but I don't remember it that way. When I saw the water and broken glass, and my companion happily slurping up the fish I'd so painstakingly raised—despite our epidemic emotionalization of them, dogs are very unsentimental characters—I knew that one part of my life was over and another had begun. I just didn't know what was ahead or that it might take decades to learn the outcome.

After the cleanup, there was little or no discussion in my family. The fish were not mourned or, as far as I can recall, missed. My guess is that my parents were relieved.

I think I knew, on some level, that I had to move beyond those gurgling confines, and might not have been able to do it on my own. I haven't owned a fish since, nor wanted to. I eventually left the cemetery behind, too. My involvement with nature seemed to end with the collapse of my fish empire. Yet, clearly, I was wrong. My need for nature wasn't finished; it was a memory, an experience embedded in my subconscious, simply waiting to come to life again. Perhaps waiting for a dog, a disturbed border collie, to awaken it.

Today my life is enveloped by nature, by what I can call ecstatic experiences. Instead of fish, I have dogs, donkeys, sheep, chickens. Instead of tanks, I have barns. Watering systems have replaced filters as a concern; hay has replaced fish food. I still breed animals, and sometimes they die. My dogs live in a world at least partly constructed for them, a landscape of fences, sheep, streams, and paths.

I walk miles in deep woods each day, help the farrier care for the donkeys' hooves, share this place not only with my farm animals and dogs but with raccoons, coyotes, skunks, weasels, chipmunks, bats, foxes, countless birds, hordes of bugs and snakes. The boy who hated summer camp would be astonished. I still can't name most of the flowers growing in my gardens, or the varieties of bushes and trees that surround me. I can hardly distinguish one bird from another. A farmer friend was excited last summer to see several Baltimore orioles dancing around an old tree near my driveway, a rare sight. I hadn't noticed.

Only recently have I begun to understand that we can experience nature in different ways, come to it from entirely different perspectives. Nature isn't found only in the wild.

At Bedlam Farm, my moments and memories include having breakfast with Paula on the front porch, taking the sheep to the pasture on a moonlit night, watching the chickens peck their way across the grass, sitting in front of the crackling woodstove on a dark, still winter's night.

Sometimes such moments are passive: watching black

thunderclouds roll in from miles away, listening to raucous birdsong. Sometimes they are active: maneuvering a tiny lamb out from its struggling mother, finding and eating fresh eggs in the morning, wading with Clementine into brooks and streams. I can sit for hours watching coyotes prowl or a hawk circling, hunting mice and snakes.

My soul mate on this journey has been Orson. He brought me here. He stands with me here. Dogs are emotive, affectionate, and stimulating far beyond the capacity of the brightest-colored fish. A life with dogs—since they are animals, not human—is always an encounter with nature, no matter where it occurs, one that quite frequently connects us to our pasts. They're simple creatures, but they provide sensory diversity, opportunities for discovery and imagination, both connection and solitude—they are certainly radioactive jewels of memory.

The ability of an adult to look upon the world with wonder is an essential instrument in the work of the poet, the artist, the creative thinker. Edith Cobb, who often wrote about the imaginative experiences of childhood, said that wonder is the genesis of all knowledge.

My fish and now my dog Orson may not be able to experience a sense of wonder, but they can evoke it in me. That could be one of Orson's most meaningful gifts—and yet another reason to see him and other dogs as animals, not humans. The more like us they seem, the less of a bridge to nature they are.

"Let's go for a ride," I yelled to the dogs on a hot and sticky July afternoon. I'd been working all day, and suddenly, I was tired and discouraged. Sometimes I get sick of sitting at a computer, sick of myself. I miss my wife and daughter and the ease of life in New York City and Jersey.

Anthony and his crew had finished the Dog Room and moved on to other jobs elsewhere. I was glad to have more peace and quiet, but of course I missed them. This is one reason I love dogs: they will not go off to college, tire of my mood swings, or take new jobs. On the other hand, they cannot talk or understand my weariness. A wave of sorrow passed over me.

I opened the back door and the dogs rushed out. Clem was happy to go anywhere, Orson just wanted to go with me. Only Rose stopped to see what we were doing. Heading for sheep? Riding the ATV? Walking across the road to the meadow?

Let's take the ATV, I decided. A trip for Orson and me. I left Rose and Clementine on the porch; they were disappointed, but they would get over it.

I pulled the cover off the machine and Orson hopped up onto the backseat. The engine roared to life and we headed up the slope, along the fence, over the top of the hill. Orson navigated intently over my shoulder.

I steered the ATV off the trail and, for the first time, into the woods at the crest of the hill, deeper and farther than I'd gone before, beyond my own property and through a thick stand of pine. I saw by the stone fences and rusting wire that this was once pasture.

It occurred to me that if any mishap should befall us up here, no one could even guess where to look. The ride got rougher, my face catching tree branches, the ATV bouncing over rocks and logs. Still, I kept going.

Suddenly, we hit a clearing; I turned off the engine.

I walked over to a boulder and sat down. Orson sniffed

and circled. It had been brutally hot for days, but it was cooler up here, and damp from a thunderstorm the day before.

I had no clear idea where I was or how to get back. From the sun, though, I could pick a general direction. Eventually I would see something I recognized. In the worst case, I could simply retrace the ATV tracks, so long as I returned before dark. I'd learned a few things from my time in the country.

Sunbeams streaked through the trees. Orson lay in front of me, keeping me company. "What a great creature you are," I told him. Orson came over to me, gave me his paw, licked my face; he always gives the impression, true or not, that he gets it.

I was standing outside myself and felt a curious sensation, as if I were suddenly immune from pain, impervious to loss. My leg did not ache. I was neither old nor young, only there, at this place, in this moment, alone in the woods but not lonely. I was surrounded by life itself. And accompanied by this dog.

It seems important—for their sakes—to understand and accept what dogs and other animals can do and what they can't. People told me all the time that they wished they could follow my lead, that I was living out their dreams on this farm with dogs I love, experiencing their fantasies, creating a perfect life. How strange, I often thought. Nobody knows what another person's life is like; nobody ought to glibly wish to trade places.

I was a very lucky man, I knew. My thinking about ecstatic places had helped me understand who I was and how I got to be here; it also reminded me that I could, in fact, step outside myself.

But not too often, and never for very long. Soon enough, inexorably, the strange and lonely little boy returns.

I wished I could reach across time and speak to him. I wished I could tell him that things would get better. He might be pleased to know that one day he would own a rolling farm with four barns and three loving dogs and donkeys and sheep and chickens.

I whistled for my dog Orson, and he jumped up into my lap, and showered me with kisses. How could he possibly know? How could he possibly understand? Why, then, did it seem so clear to me that he did?

CHAPTER EIGHT

Sirius

Summer came, hot, humid, and buggy, day after day. Even the border collies dragged a bit, slowed down, took rests in the shade. On the farm, life quieted to a whisper once the sun launched itself into the cloudless, windless sky.

It was the kind of moist heat that made showering almost irrelevant: Once you walked outside, you were sweat-soaked. The sheep camped under a big pine tree in the pasture, and the donkeys hugged the inside of the barn. There was little traffic. The only creatures that seemed up and about were the flies, merciless and ubiquitous.

By late morning, we'd retreated onto the porch or into the farmhouse, where the enormous windows seemed to draw in a bit of breeze.

"Dog days," people said when you met them at the variety store or passed at the post office, wiping their faces.

Though I'd heard the term all my life, nobody I knew could say precisely what the phrase meant, or where the idea came from. I'd always imagined it originated in the South and pictured torpid curs lying around during the nastiest days of July and August, when even dogs couldn't bring themselves to move.

The truth, I discovered, was richer.

Thousands of years ago, when the night sky was unobscured by artificial light and smog, the Romans, among others, drew images in the sky by connecting the bright dots they saw above them.

These star pictures are the constellations, and at night, when the dogs and I walk into the meadow or to the top of the pasture and look up, I think of those ancient people and feel connected to them. Many of them probably had sheep and donkeys too, and were smelling the same things I was.

They saw in the sky what was important in their lives. Some saw images of bears (Ursa Major and Ursa Minor) or a bull (Taurus). Perhaps significantly, they named one group of stars Canis Major, the big dog. And they named the brightest star in that constellation—it's also the brightest star in the night sky—Sirius.

Anthropologists believe that the human-canine bond probably began thousands of years ago. Perhaps wolves were drawn to humans' settlements and their campfires, and people threw them some bones and food. Perhaps people found a wolf puppy, brought him into their camp and raised him. Maybe it developed this way: The humans provided shelter and food, and the wolves companionship, protection, help with hunting.

The Romans, closer than I am to that original wolf by the campfire, crammed their writings and drawings with references to dogs—house pets, guard animals, hunters, and herders. Generals rode into battles with dogs; the rich kept them as pets; shepherds relied on them to protect their flocks. Clearly, the human-canine bond was well under way when it came time to name the stars.

Sirius is bright, in part because it is so luminous, twenty-three times brighter than the sun; but also because it is so close (for a star), just 8.6 light-years away. The Romans must have thought a great deal of their dogs to name this star after them.

Sirius shines so brightly that the Romans thought the earth received heat from it. The word comes from the Greek for "searing" or "scorching." Since in summer the Dog Star rises and sets with the sun, the Romans believed that the hot weather of this period—from July 3 to August 11—was caused by Sirius, in concert with the sun. Sirius was, to them, a mischievous star. Thus, the sultry dog days.

During the dog days that summer, I began waking at four-thirty, and, instead of lying in bed, listening to the birds, I often pulled on my jeans and a shirt and slipped outside with Orson.

Clem didn't usually wake up; she was happy to stay in bed, curled up next to Paula. Rose darted her head out of whatever room she'd made her lair when she heard me stirring, but when I waved her off, she vanished. She would rather herd sheep than go look at a star, anyway.

Orson, as ever, was excited to go with me. A born navigator and adventurer, he was up for anything, anytime, so long as I was along.

We stepped quietly out the back door, usually confronting Winston and his hens already on the prowl for grubs and worms. I climbed onto the ATV, turned on the headlights, released the choke, warmed up the engine, and we headed out. How lucky I was to be living in a place where there are few neighbors to disturb.

If I'd thought about it and brewed a pot of coffee the night before, I poured some into an aluminum travel mug and fastened it to the front of the ATV with a bungee cord. I might bring along a banana or apple, and a snack for Orson.

He was usually already waiting on the ATV seat. He leaned into me, his nose nestled along the right side of my neck or on my shoulder. We chugged to the top of the pasture, a bit of a thrill as there were ditches, puddles, farm debris, and roaming animals, all sometimes hard to see, even with headlights, in the predawn grayness.

The donkeys, quietly monitoring as they always do, picked up on the routine. Most mornings, when I rumbled up, they were waiting for me at the corner of the pasture. I slowed, let the engine idle, and reached into my pockets for the donkey cookies I usually carried around. I scratched each girl on the nose or kissed her forehead, and left them munching peacefully. The sheep wanted no part of this and usually remained clustered together in the grass, lying in a tight circle.

We rumbled over the path that runs across the top of the pasture, into the deep woods with its remnants of stone fences and its scrawny trees, surely a pasture once, part of an earlier farm. From a clearing—the same one Orson and I had discovered earlier—you could see across the Black Creek Valley, well into Vermont, when the sun rose.

When I turned off the ATV, the forest resounded at first with quiet. Sometimes I saw startled deer bounding off. Orson, who would chase almost anything, was for some reason uninterested in deer. Nothing about this dog was consistent or straightforward.

I sat on a boulder and gazed upward, sipping my coffee, eating my apple, looking for Sirius, the Dog Star, as the eastern sky began to redden. It felt like much of my life had led me to this place, in search of this star.

And there it was, right above me.

Just as the Internet astronomers and star buffs had promised, Sirius was impossible to miss. "Just look up," one of them had e-mailed me, "and you will find it. Or it will find you."

Stargazers call Sirius the "champion of the twinklers," but I had never really looked at it before, I don't think. It's the luminary of Canis Major and represents Orion the Hunter's larger hunting dog; that's why it has become known as the Dog Star.

It was, in fact, luminous. It did twinkle. I could only imagine what it must have looked like thousands of years ago, when nothing on the ground competed with it and the sky was not veiled by pollutants and smoke. Something about it felt personal, not only because of the dog connection, but because it seemed aimed right at Orson and me, shining directly down on us. At this moment, I felt what people might have felt thousands of years ago: This was my star, our star, close enough to touch.

Orson plopped down next to me. "Look, pal," I murmured. "We're so lucky. We had a star and we didn't know it."

Orson

CHAPTER NINE

In the Garden

My farm was roughly 170 years old, filled with echoes and traces of the past—long-buried wallpaper, the tracings on the walls of old stairs and stoves, bits of broken plates and pipes that rose from the soil after a storm. It's difficult enough to maintain and navigate now, so I'm in awe of the energy and will of the people who built it, piece by piece. Somewhere along the line, someone planted the gardens that encircle the house.

I planted one myself. The "Victory Garden," I called it, the concrete base of a now-vanished silo I laboriously filled up with donkey and sheep manure, hundreds of cubic feet of soil, mulch, and dead animals. I filled it with an unplanned jumble of flowers, annuals and perennials I couldn't even name, and took great pleasure in the riotous color they brought that corner of the barnyard.

But the gardens grew difficult to maintain, especially for somebody with gimpy legs, so I hired a group of local women who love trees and plants and who tended to the cultivating and weeding and pruning that were beyond my abilities.

Hard workers, they came once a week in summer to turn over the soil, work in organic fertilizers, run drip hoses, and plant fresh seedlings. It took months of brutish work in the sun, but they'd done a wonderful job; I loved seeing Bedlam Farm's gardens thrive and flourish.

On Tuesdays, Sarah and Wendy would pull up in a Subaru, armed with shovels, bags of cow manure, garden tools, and bottled water. Sarah was a student at Bennington and Wendy took odd jobs, most related to the outdoors.

They worked steadily and quietly, and broke around noon for a quick lunch. They loved the dogs, who returned their affections and were delighted to hang out with them. Even Rose came over for a brief sniff and pat once in a while.

I always asked if the dogs were bothering them and offered to bring them inside, but Sarah and Wendy were dismayed, even outraged, at the thought. Clementine usually ended up in Wendy's lap; Rose retreated to the far side of the yard to watch; and Orson quickly turned Sarah into one of his girlfriends. She was very fond of him. When she came into the yard, he ran up, tail wagging, to slurp at her face. Then he rolled on his back to have his tummy scratched.

To me, this friendship was one of the signs that Orson was coming around. Another was the ATV, which had become his passion, purpose, and work. Curiously, the soul retriever was right: he'd needed work, and finding it seemed to be anchoring him.

Things seemed to be working. Our morning treks to see the Dog Star couldn't have been more peaceful or beautiful for me—and perhaps for him. It was something else we could do together, something else for him to feel happy and successful about.

Meanwhile, our calming and grounding training continued, along with regular visits to Vermont for chiropractic and acupuncture. I still sprinkled herbs into his food every day. And except on the hottest days, we also continued our rudimentary herding training; Orson still liked running in circles around the sheep in their pen.

I had the unprecedented feeling that I'd found the key to this dog; that training, hard work, experimentation, and the opportunities offered by the farm were slowly and painstakingly healing him. I was doing nearly everything that I could and should be doing. To do more seemed inappropriate, even excessive, but to do less would be a violation of our covenant.

Orson had work. He was benefiting from persistent and positive training. The two of us had things to do together. As Rose had a role, now, so did he. There were actually long periods of the day when he seemed quite at ease, and didn't annoy me or wreak havoc.

Another first. For as long as I'd loved Orson, I couldn't remember so much success, progress on so many fronts. Sometimes I looked at him, curled on my foot while I wrote, and thought: Perhaps I've reached some of those broken parts. Perhaps I've helped to repair some of them.

My soul mate seemed to be finding his place in the world; finally, and at long last, it seemed to be making some sense to him. This was immensely satisfying, uplifting. Often, despairing at the misery and suffering in the world, I nearly gave up on the idea that any of it could be reversed. So Orson's improvement served as something of a hopeful symbol.

He, of course, was doing a great deal for me, as well:

watching out for me, serving as my muse, my guardian, my pal. During those weeks when Paula was working back in New Jersey, he was always—*always*—there. Unlike Paula, he admired everything I said or did, approved of every word I wrote. He walked with me through the world.

One Tuesday, as I was writing and the dogs were out with Sarah and Wendy, I heard a scream and sounds of confusion and concern from the front yard. I came out onto the porch, and saw Sarah holding a bloody handkerchief to her right shoulder. Her T-shirt had been torn from her shoulder.

She was upset, and Wendy was tending to her. Orson looked confused, even abashed. I came running out and asked what had happened.

She had been stroking and petting Orson who was lying next to her, Sarah said; she decided to get up and move to another section of the garden. As she stood, he leaped up and bit her just below the neck, at the collarbone.

It was not a deep wound, but certainly a wound. I could see the blood and the welts. In a few moments, bruising would begin to appear.

I brought Orson into the house. In the bathroom, we applied antibiotic cream and bandaged Sarah's wound. I offered to take her to the doctor's office, but she refused, dismissing the attack. It was not a big deal, she said; she'd been bitten before, even by her own family dog. She loved Orson; she was sure he hadn't meant any harm. It was probably her fault, she said; she must have stood up too quickly, moved erratically, provoked him in some way.

I appreciated her love of Orson and her generosity of spirit, but I told her I didn't see it that way. This was not her fault; she was not responsible. It was a disturbing, even frightening, experience, and I was terribly sorry about it.

At my urging, she came over several times in the next few weeks to work with Orson. She brought him food and treats, walked him, petted him. Slightly anxious at first, she overcame that, and made sure to move slowly when Orson was around. For his part, he remained always happy to see her, friendly, appropriate, eager to visit with her and lie nearby. Sarah graciously continued to work with Orson around.

But I was shaken. He'd never bitten anyone like that before. I had no obvious explanation. It was certainly possible that Sarah's sudden movement provoked some herding response in him, but this was not a nip, it was a bite, inches from her throat. He had drawn blood, torn clothes, left welts and bruises. This was an attack on a human being, the first by any of my dogs. I had no ready understanding of it.

Neither did any of my growing circle of vets, trainers, holistic practitioners, advisors, and shamans.

Two weeks later, a nine-year-old walking down the road to play basketball at the Presbyterian church reached over the fence to pet Clementine, and Orson rushed up and went for his left hand, not injuring him or tearing flesh, but ripping his sleeve. Like Anthony, this boy was a country kid, and dogs that nipped or bit were not unusual to him, but he was obviously frightened.

I called his parents, offered to replace the shirt, offered profuse apologies. I had no temptation to blame this kid. Sure, he shouldn't have reached over the fence, but what kid wouldn't want to pet Clementine, who loved it whenever anyone did? The responsibility was mine; so was the shock and bewilderment.

After that, Orson was not allowed in the front yard if I

wasn't there with him. I kept him either in the back fenced run or in the house.

Some days after the incident with the boy, a man who lived nearby came to ask for permission to hunt on my property during deer season. Almost everyone in town had welcomed me and made me feel at home, but this man made his dislike of flatlanders and outsiders—people like me—quite well known. He made it clear he didn't approve of me, the changes I'd made to the farm, or my existence in general. I wasn't crazy about him, either. We had no quarrels or troubles, but neither were we close or friendly. But he was a good and honest man, and I would be happy to give him permission to hunt.

He pulled up on a big tractor he'd been using to do some work on his property. Orson was out in the back run. I heard the tractor's noise, then wild barking, and had an awful feeling. I ran out the back door. Orson had bitten him deeply. The man's shirt was torn almost completely off his body; blood was trickling down his chest from a wound right next to his throat.

I pulled Orson inside and apologized to my neighbor, who'd only thought to pat a dog over the kennel fence. For all of our previous coolness, he didn't blame the dog or even seem particularly angry. One of the many things I enjoy about people in the country is their love of animals, including dogs, and their visceral understanding that trouble will sometimes happen. They rarely sue or make much fuss, which I appreciated.

But an anxious dread came over me. In the years that he'd been with me, I hadn't once, even for a second, believed that Orson was a violent or dangerous dog. The thought hadn't entered my mind. He was the Big Nipper, sure, an obnoxious pain in the ass, a dog who might put a tear in the cuff of your jeans. But not a dog who would cause injury. I'd never dreamed that he could harm a human being the way he had this man.

I had romanticized, personified, mythologized, and rationalized, and I couldn't any longer. Now I knew Orson was capable of harming people—a friend like Sarah, a kid walking by, a neighbor coming to the house. This after all of the examinations, the socializing, the training, the herding, the acupuncture and herbs and shamanic retrievals. I felt my heart race with fear.

I understood too clearly that things couldn't ever be the same. Before, I could tell myself that Orson wouldn't harm anybody. But I could no longer say to some child whom Orson bit, whose face was marred by stitches or scars, that I didn't know it might happen—because now I did.

It was a jarring reminder of the limits of training, knowledge, patience, of love itself. I've never worked harder at anything in my life than I had at training my troubled dog, and the incidents in the garden had reminded me of what I should have known all along: Orson was an animal, and parts of him were beyond my reach.

I have a powerful vision of what a life with dogs should be; I've written books and columns about it, given hundreds of talks about it to people of good faith. And I was not ambivalent. Dogs should not harm people, I'd said a thousand times. If there is any rule involving dogs, it is that we are responsible for them. Every time a dog bites a person, especially a child, the life of every dog is threatened.

I cursed the gardens. Every attack had happened in or near a garden.

In all my life with dogs, many of them, I'd never seen a more dreadful, painful sight than my neighbor's bloodied chest. After the man left, I brought Orson into the house and sat and rocked him in my arms. I closed my eyes and held him tightly to me. "What have you done?" I asked him over and over. "What have you done?" He looked at me inquisitively, sensing my emotion but not understanding it. He seemed concerned about me, licking my hands and face. Perhaps he saw more than I did.

Then I asked myself the even more painful question, but perhaps the right one: What had I failed to do?

Orson

CHAPTER TEN

Choices

I had four choices.

I could ask Anthony to construct a more secure kennel for Orson behind the house, away from traffic and visitors, a place that nobody could reach into, that Orson couldn't get over or around.

I could find a more isolated and peaceful home for him, where there were fewer people, fewer vehicles, fewer gates and boundaries and fewer things coming through them.

I could take Orson to a specialist at a veterinary school like Cornell or the University of Pennsylvania for more sophisticated testing—MRIs, brain scans, further blood work and X-rays—to make certain that no medical issue, a tumor, for example, or some neurological injury, was causing this violent behavior.

I could bring him to my vet and have him killed.

The next morning, Orson and I rode up at five a.m. on the ATV to see Sirius. He assumed his navigating position from the backseat. The sky was too cloudy to see the Dog Star clearly, and the sun rose already shrouded in haze. I could tell the day would be sticky and warm. I sat munching a piece of toast, tossing him biscuits and scratching him under his chin, his favorite spot.

Dogs, dogs. One day he is biting somebody on the neck, the next morning he's sitting up on this beautiful hilltop with me, gentle as a kitten.

"What are we going to do with you, my friend?" I asked.

I considered the first option. Anthony could easily build a secure kennel, with thick fence posts, behind the farmhouse. If the fences were high enough, nobody could reach in. Anthony might even build two fences and electrify the outer one. There would be room enough inside to give Orson space to run, and a vantage point from which to watch the sheep and the house, but no one could get near him.

Orson, I knew, would hate it. He always wanted to be near me, always wanted to be a part of things. He would be barking and peering anxiously out all the time, looking for me.

I would hate it, too. I loved being with Orson; I didn't bring him into my life in order to keep him isolated much of the day. He was a social creature and loved stimulation and interaction.

"I could build it," Anthony told me. "And nobody could get into it, and he couldn't get out. But it wouldn't be a kennel, it would be a prison. Just so you know." I did know.

Weeks earlier, I had driven by Comstock Prison, north of my farm; it had two fences, too.

This was not why I had this dog, or any dog.

As I mulled, Orson tore off into the woods, through the mist, after his first chipmunk of the day. Whenever Orson ran into the woods, I could hear alarmed squeaks echoing through the trees. Then he started digging furiously at some groundhog hole, mounds of dirt piling up behind him. Poor guy, I thought. Always looking for the right work, never quite finding it.

What if I could locate some remote farm where there would be space for him to run, woods to explore, and someone who would be happy to take in a dog like this? Some farmers might treasure a dog like Orson, and give him a good home. But I would worry about him forever, think of him constantly, miss him always. More important, I'd only be trying to slip off the hook.

Obviously, there are circumstances where it's quite appropriate to give a dog away—I'd done it, not long before. But I would still feel, and be, irresponsible if I just passed a problem dog along. If he bit another kid or another adult, perhaps more seriously, a few inches higher, attacked someone's face or eyes—could I live with that? Should I?

I was choking on my own statistics, those I'd spouted in my writings and in talks all over the country: nearly five million people are bitten by dogs each year. Hundreds of thousands, more than half of them children, are hurt seriously enough to go to a hospital. Talk to any emergency-room pediatrician if you want to know what a dog can do to a kid. I have talked to several.

Dogs that bite are likely to do it again. Dog lovers don't like to deal with this issue, for obvious and understandable reasons. But to me, dogs that harm people violate the fundamental understanding between humans and canines. Dogs that bite cause lawsuits, insurance problems, restrictions on the movement of all dogs, and a lot of human pain and suffering. Keeping a violent dog is antithetical to everything I believe about a life with dogs; passing one along to someone else was no better. No, I could not give Orson away and then simply hope for the best.

It really came down to this: Wasn't it selfish of me to value my love for a dog over the safety and welfare of other human beings? Didn't that distort the history and nature of dogs, their place in our lives? Orson was not more important to me than the safety of a child. At least, I didn't want him to be.

The third option was perhaps the most feasible. Go to Cornell, spend five or six thousand dollars (I'd checked) for the elaborate workups necessary to determine if there was any hidden physical factor—a brain tumor, perhaps—causing this aggressive behavior. One vet had suggested Orson might, when aroused, be experiencing something akin to seizures.

Such tests might or might not find something, however. They would be expensive, frightening, and painful for him, draining for me. I had exhausted the possibilities of conventional veterinary care and much of alternative medicine as well. My kitchen counters were stacked with Chinese herbs; Orson had been punctured by countless needles. I could rescue fifty dogs for the cost of one trip to a specialist.

I had bought a farm and stocked it with sheep partly because of Orson, trained him faithfully in the heat and cold and wet. I'd employed truckloads of treats, spent thousands of hours repeating grounding, calming, and obedience commands. We'd even gotten a herding ribbon together.

What was the outer limit of what was appropriate to do for a dog? How much money was too much to spend? How much time was too much time? How much emotional energy should anyone invest?

Living in this hamlet upstate, I'd come closer than ever to the grinding poverty people struggled with. There was Margaret down the hill, dying of cancer, living alone with her three cats. Neighbors dropped off meals on her porch, since she was too prideful to accept food for free.

A family up the road lived in a trailer with gaping holes covered by tarpaper. Teenagers came to my door every week, practically begging for work. Hollow-eyed hunters came, desperate for permission to hunt—not for sport, but for food for their families. I knew of dogs that had been shot because their owners couldn't afford veterinary care.

Where was the balance between the care and money I lavished on Orson, and the needs and attentions of human beings that lived within my sight and consciousness, and beyond? I didn't know, but viscerally and instinctively, I felt I was approaching the line, perhaps had already crossed it.

No, it didn't seem right to subject this dog to more tests, to spend thousands of dollars seeking answers I might never find. I cherished the dogs in my life, in part because they lived with and served us so willingly and faithfully.

When the role of dogs gets distorted or confused, if we fail to put any boundaries on our love for them, then we've torn the fabric that so closely connects us. My dogs will never be on ventilators in canine intensive-care units, or live beyond their time, or take the place of human beings. That's my ethic, not a prescription for anybody else. We all have to make our own choices.

Suddenly, I had to make mine.

That left the final choice: putting to death a dog that I loved dearly, that had changed my life, that I'd written books and articles about, that was known and loved by many people beyond me. I owed him so much.

I was afraid even to talk to my vet Mary about the prospect of euthanizing Orson. I imagined her shocked and outraged that I would even consider such a thing, and pictured her refusing to put Orson down, throwing me out of her office, forcing me to find a less ethical vet who would do it for the money, no questions asked. I had the names of a couple of those.

I could even hear her words: "We don't kill animals like Orson. He's wonderful. He's healthy. How dare you even ask?" She loved all kinds of animals. She loved Orson, too, and always asked about him. Wouldn't she be horrified?

After we rode back down to the house, I called her and asked if I could visit. She said to come right over.

She seemed puzzled when I showed up solo, without a dog, but waved me back into her small office. I sat on a bench. I remember a painting of a proud Dalmatian hovering above us while we talked, for an hour, about Orson.

She already knew about his arousal and nipping, of course. Now I told her about the incidents, the bites, the blood and torn shirts. She understood what I was feeling, she said. She had had to put down an aggressive dog of her own.

We went over, in detail, all the possibilities. Orson might well have some tumor or other medical problem, she said. But conventional care hadn't found it, and holistic treatments hadn't eliminated it. She told me what I might expect if I went to specialists or veterinary behaviorists, what they would do, what they might find, what it might cost.

Sending him to another home was a possibility, and Mary agreed to look around for one. But she agreed that I would, essentially, be passing a serious problem on to others.

She wasn't telling me what to do, but she said her practice—a loving, responsible, and ethical one— did not believe in circulating dogs that harmed humans. She believed that violent dogs ought to be put down, and if I sincerely believed Orson was one, if I had serious reason to believe he would hurt more people, she would help me.

"In the final analysis," Mary said, "you know your dog best. Only you can really decide. I will support you."

It nearly brought me to tears to hear that. I couldn't ask for more. My vet was telling me she trusted me to make this decision; it meant a lot.

I went home to think, take a walk and decide. Strolling behind the house, I looked up at the sky, at the spot where the Dog Star would appear in the morning. Pretty, but useless.

I called Lesley the shaman. This was not her terrain, and I didn't really want any visions or communications. But, strangely, she had become a friend, one I felt knew Orson's spirit, so I just wanted her to know what was happening. She had no advice, one of the reasons I liked her. Some things belonged in the spirit realm, some in the human domain, and she respected the difference. The attacks sounded awful and serious, she said. I was right to take them seriously. So even the shaman was out of ideas.

Everyone around me—especially Paula—grasped that this was my decision to make. Initially, she'd been horrified by the havoc and expense this dog had caused, but she had come to love him, and vice versa. She'd rarely seen the aggression that was causing all this trouble, just the sweetheart who slept at the foot of the bed and slurped our faces each morning. Put Orson down? "Could you really do that?" she wondered. Emma urged me to go slowly, wondered if there was anything else to try.

One close friend urged me not to kill Orson. "It would be a mistake. You would regret it. Keep working with him." But this was not advice I either sought or needed, however well-meaning.

The truth was, I wasn't really soliciting opinions, and the people who knew me well were not offering any.

It was up to me, my vet had said. There might be more alternatives. Her practice did not like to kill healthy, well-adjusted animals. But she knew how much I loved Orson, how hard I had worked to help and train him. If I chose to put him down, she would either come to my farm to do it or set up a private time at the clinic.

So, suddenly, there we were. Four choices, none of them good.

I've often found myself alone when in trouble. I turn inward, pulling myself almost into a ball, trying to reason through what must be done.

But I have also come to rely on the thinking and writings of a few people who've touched or inspired or guided me. I carry their books when I travel, keep them stacked around me at home. They never quite tell me what to do, but always help me figure it out. I call them my secret board of directors.

It's a very distinguished membership. Thomas Merton, the late Trappist monk and writer, serves on the board. So does Abraham Lincoln, whose moral clarity and humanity led him through choices so much more awful than any I would ever face.

When it came to moral choices, the process by which one makes them or doesn't, I always read and reread Hannah Arendt, the philosopher. I especially cherished *Responsibility and Judgment,* a series of writings about right and wrong and how each of us decides which is which. I've often turned to this book when I have rough choices to make, and it has never failed to help me.

So I settled on the porch with Orson and read one of Arendt's chapters on moral conduct. It was a soft, warm late afternoon and the hawks were circling slowly over the meadow in front of the farmhouse. Orson was dozing on the porch near me, Rose sitting by the fence, eyeing the sheep. Clementine was lying on the grass on her back, snoring contentedly.

It was terribly discouraging to have made it through these five-plus decades, to struggle to get to this place with Orson's great help and inspiration, to be living on this farm, sitting on this beautiful porch on a sweet, lazy summer afternoon, and be thinking about this awful act.

Winston the rooster hopped over the fence and came to sit next to Orson, as he often did in the afternoon. I heard the donkeys braying softly from the barn, where they'd taken refuge from the heat, reminding me that a cookie or two would be appreciated. I felt old, weary, and sad. And lonely. I might soon be lonelier still.

So I read. Moral conduct, Arendt wrote, depends mostly on the discussions we have with ourselves. We must not contradict ourselves by making exceptions in our own favor; we must not place ourselves in positions in which we would have to despise ourselves. Morally speaking, this should enable us not only to tell right from wrong, but also to do right and avoid wrong.

I found the passage I was looking for. "It certainly is not a matter of concern with the other but with the self, not of meekness but of human dignity and even human pride," she'd written. "The standard is neither the love of some neighbor nor self-love, but self-respect."

It did not matter what other people, or other dog lovers, would have done or would think of what I decided. It mattered what I thought of myself; the respect I needed to seek was my own.

The world is filled with people of certainty, of strong opinions, who have a sure sense of what others ought to do. Nowhere were they more numerous than in the vast network of people and institutions that constitute the dog culture. I often met people who were very sure about everything. Housebreak the dog this way. Train the dog that way. Always do this, never that.

Yet if my life with dogs had taught me anything, it was to be less, not more, certain. The more I knew them, the less confident I was about what made dogs tick. Animals have ways of teaching you that for all your books, vets, websites, shamans, and holistic practitioners, you are not in control. Animals live in their own sphere, by their own lights.

There was a preacher I met, a few miles south of here, who walked the hills and valleys, looking to save souls; I was fond of him, admired his energy and faith. He'd never saved a single soul in all those years of walking, he told me, but he never missed a day of trying.

He always loved my dogs, liked to pat and talk to them. He used to stop by my little mountaintop cabin once or twice a year, often in winter, to inquire about my soul, and although he didn't get far with me, he usually stayed for a cup of tea. We talked for a few minutes while he rested and gathered himself up for the rest of his arduous day.

I thought of him that afternoon, and wished he would come along. At some point during every visit, he used to say that the devil was the world's best theologian, because he knew right and wrong better than anyone. I would have liked to meet somebody that sure.

Instead, I was the sole preacher, legislator, and theologian of my world. I thought of all the people I could call, consult, agonize with—but I stopped. The only person I had to ask was me, sitting right there beside my dog.

What pushed me through my lethargy was a beautiful passage Arendt cited from Immanuel Kant, so apt on that summer afternoon, close to the end of the dog days, that it chilled me despite the heat: "Two things fill the mind with ever new and increasing admiration and awe, the oftener and more steadily we reflect on them: the starry heaven above me and the moral law within me."

Orson and I had been under the starry heavens all summer and now, I had to listen to the moral law within me.

I called my vet.

Orson and Clem

CHAPTER ELEVEN

Sleepaway

It was the third of August, deep into the dog days. There were only eight left. We would not see Sirius rise with the sun again for another year. Orson would not see it again at all, at least not with me.

I needed to screen things out. How much I loved him. How much other people loved him. How integral a part of my life he was. How much we had done together. How much he had done for me. How much fun we'd had and how much trouble he'd gotten into.

That he had become, to many people, a symbol of human beings keeping faith with their dogs. That people had told me how, in one way or another, our contract had moved them to make and keep their own. That his death, consequently, would sadden and anger people and might discourage some.

That I would always wonder if I had done the right thing.

That I would miss him. That Orson was my lifetime dog, and I was not likely to have another.

That I would lose my guardian, my guide, whom I'd failed in the ultimate, most profound, way. I was breaking the covenant that had bound us together for years and altered much of my life.

I put these thoughts aside, the agonizing and doubt, because the decision was made. I would live with it. Or not.

My vet, Mary, sensitive to these sorrows and worries, offered to come to the farm to euthanize Orson there. I decided against it. I didn't want him to die here; I didn't want to associate the farm with Orson's death. He'd been to the vet's office many times and felt comfortable with her. And I wanted him to have the safety of a professional facility, just in case something went wrong. I would be there with him.

I called Anthony and asked that he arrange to dig a grave at the top of the pasture, on the crest of the hill, from which Orson could keep an eye on things. I asked him to find a mason to cut Orson's name into a block of rough fieldstone, to place on the grave.

And I asked him to make sure no one was around the place in the afternoon.

Within a couple of hours, the grave stood ready; the stone was cut and placed next to it. And nobody was there. In summer, the farm can be eerily still in the afternoon; the animals shut down in the heat and wait for sunset to move and forage.

One last ride.

"Let's hit the ATV," I yelled to Orson, and he bounded happily onto his seat. We tore up the hill, right past the hole in the ground, and up into the woods where we'd often sat and waited for Sirius, the Dog Star. I sat down on the usual rock and he hopped into my arms. I hugged him long and hard, he licked me several times, then plopped down for a scratch, his head on my foot.

"Thanks for rescuing me from New Jersey and technology books," I said. It was all there was to say.

We rode back down the hill, then drove to the veterinary clinic. Our appointment was for five p.m., the last of the day, when most of the employees were gone, along with all the clients. There were only a couple of cars in the parking lot.

Mary was waiting for me by the side door, so I didn't have to go through the waiting room. She had needles ready on the examining table. She said little, other than to tell me that she had once made the same decision herself for one of her dogs, and she supported mine. She told me not to worry about the bill, that it would be sent. I realize now that it never was.

It was a small, spotless, antiseptic examining room. I sat on the floor. Orson, anxious, crawled into my lap. Mary asked if I was ready, and I nodded yes. She was exquisitely professional and sensitive, knowing exactly when to speak and when not to.

Orson put his head on my right shoulder, his body resting against my chest, and stared into my eyes, trembling a bit. He licked my face, and I stroked his head. Mary inserted one needle into his left foreleg.

Then she administered a powerful sedative, a mix of acepromazine and Torbugesic. Very quickly, he licked my chin, then sagged, and his eyes began to close. I kissed his nose and face and hugged him for dear life.

Then Mary administered the drug Sleepaway, to stop his heart. My right hand cradled his head and shoulders, my left was on his chest, right next to Mary's stethoscope. I could feel his heart slow, then stop.

"He's gone," Mary said, listening carefully through her

stethoscope. She gave me a heavy canvas bag and together we placed his body inside and carried it to my truck.

It was a very sticky, hot day. I drove home, parked the pickup behind the house.

I let Rose out of the house. Rose saw everything that happened on the farm, good and bad, constantly inventorying the comings and goings. She'd lived with Orson nearly her whole life, handling him skillfully, deferring to him without becoming submissive like Homer. She should come along, I thought, for his burial.

Clementine stayed in the front yard. A sweet and loving Labrador, she was not into drama. She mostly cared about love and food; with or without Orson, she would have both.

I decided that I had to carry Orson up the hill. I would not drag his body in a bag, or put him on the ATV, or throw him in the back of a pickup. I had to carry him in my arms to his grave site.

But his body weighed nearly fifty pounds. I was soon soaked with sweat and out of breath. The bugs were all over me, and him. My bad leg began to throb.

Rose, having sniffed his body, walked quietly alongside, staying close.

I had to stop several times. My leg and back were rebelling against this load, pain shooting down into the knees, worse with each step. Before long, the leg had grown numb. Every five or ten minutes, I had to set his body on the grass and rest.

The pain—both kinds, all kinds—was almost unbearable. I considered calling Anthony for help, but took a deep breath and asked for strength.

I could do this. I owed Orson at least this much.

It took more than a half hour to struggle to the top of the hill, his body still warm in my grasp, and when I got there, I was disheartened to see that the grave was not deep enough. I feared that coyotes or other predators could dig him up, and I couldn't bear the thought. Rose sniffed the body again as it lay on the ground, and looked at me quizzically, wondering what instructions there would be.

There were none. We walked back down the hill to the barn, where I got a shovel, then slogged back up the hill with it. The ground was dry and hard—there had been little rain that summer—and it took an effort to dig a hole that seemed deep enough. I had to chip away for a long time, pulling out the larger rocks one at a time.

When I'd finished—drenched in sweat, covered in dirt, and aching badly—I leaned down, kissed Orson on the nose, and dragged his body into the grave; I no longer had the strength to pick it up. I arranged his body so that he was straight, no legs at awkward angles; it looked like he was sleeping comfortably. I closed both his eyes.

It took another while to shovel the dirt over him and level the ground. Then I dragged over the stone marker. It said simply: *Orson.*

I reached into my pocket for the poem I'd brought along. I'd read it to Orson a couple of times when the Dog Star rose at first light. The poem, by Boris Levinson, was called "Dream." I read this part:

I, a child
Try to reach the stars . . .
Sirius is so near.
I run to the nearest hill
My reach is always too short
Wait till I am a grown man!
Now, I am old and bent with years

No more running to the hill and mountain top—
Yet, a warm, steady, life-giving glow
Reaches me from Sirius . . . the unattainable.
I collect
White iridescent and evanescent starbeams
For my trip home to
Sirius the dog star.

My dogs and I communicate mostly wordlessly, it seems to me. But I felt I needed to say something. "I love you. I thank you. I'm so sorry."

I fussed with the grave for nearly half an hour, making sure it was filled in, the earth tightly packed. I was spent and felt weary. The pain in my leg was different, disturbing.

I heard the rumble of hooves and looked up to see Rose moving the sheep toward me at full speed. Some people believe dogs think like us, but Rose reminded me that they don't. She was not interested in mourning.

"Give it a rest, Rosie. Leave the sheep alone."

She stopped, looked surprised, left the sheep and came over to me. I walked down the hill with her, not looking back.

On the way down, I passed Winston, the rooster, hobbling up.

Two weeks after Orson's death, I was at the Hospital for Special Surgery in New York, receiving treatment for severe spinal stenosis. My bad leg, it turned out, wasn't a bad leg at all but a bad back, in which damaged discs pressing on nerves were causing intensifying pain.

By the time I'd finally relented to Paula's urging and sought treatment, I was unable to walk more than a few feet.

Paula spent days ferrying me to appointments, for X-rays and myelograms and MRIs, for consultations with a neurologist and a surgeon and a physiatrist—a specialist in managing pain. A couple of times, when the pain worsened, Paula wheeled me through the hospital in a wheelchair. I had passed through some portal into a world I dreaded, where I controlled nothing and felt at the mercy of everyone.

It was the very kind of life I had always sworn to avoid, as far from Bedlam as I could be. I missed the farm, the quiet, the routines, the small dramas, and the animals. I missed the community I had found, the friends I had made. I was frayed by the insurance forms and the waiting rooms, the city noise and congestion and traffic, the ice packs and pills, the pain.

It was confusing and frightening. Each doctor seemed to say a different thing, or say it in a different way, or interpret the condition differently. For relief, the physiatrist carefully injected a steroid into my spinal canal. The treatment would work for months or perhaps only for weeks, or it might not work. I would be walking soon, or I wouldn't be walking properly for a long time. I would need surgery. It might be a simple operation, or extensive. Or I might not need it at all.

On the farm, life was so regular, so elemental. The animals ate in the morning. The dogs were walked. We herded the sheep. I worked. The dogs were walked again, the animals fed once more.

I missed Orson.

In New Jersey, as I was resting between appointments, a friend called. How's the farm? he wanted to know. How are the dogs?

I told him I'd put Orson down. He was incredulous. "My God," he said. "I can't believe it. You killed Lassie." It was a New York kind of thing to say, dark, smart, cynical. And true.

Mother

Pearl

Clem

CHAPTER TWELVE

Life on the Farm

The human psyche is tricky; we see what we need to see.

I'd always thought of Orson as a guardian, a protector; I believed he was watching over me. I can't really explain why, but I felt safer with him around.

When he came, he ushered in one of the happiest and most productive periods of my life. When he died, it seemed to mark a darker time.

My back and legs were better, after treatment, but still quite painful. This was both discouraging and depressing, a new reality. Ordered to rest and recuperate, I had to hire people to do everything I loved to do and had come to the farm to do—feed the chickens, brush the donkeys, sweep out the barn, gather eggs, put out feed and grain. I even hired Annie, an animal lover from the adjacent town whom I'd dubbed the

Goat Lady of Cossayuna, to walk my dogs, something I'd never imagined I would do.

Annie had a wonderful way with animals; she even eventually charmed the reclusive Rose. She figured out that taking Rose into the pasture and letting her march the flock back and forth a few times would bring instant love. And of course, Clementine loved everybody, especially Annie, who took her swimming in the creek. Still, it was a wrench to see the dogs go walking off with someone else.

Other troubles seemed to follow through the fall and into the winter. The donkeys got abscesses in their hooves and were lame for a while. A powerful rainstorm created a flood that swept through the pasture and damaged the barn. One of my ewes took sick and died.

One morning, walking gingerly out to the barn, I discovered Winston lying motionless on the concrete floor, his head drooping. My friend Carr said he would bring his ax. I went to the house to get my rifle instead. Either way, we'd give him a quick death without suffering.

But Annie happened to swoop into the driveway just then. You do not shoot an animal with Annie around. She picked Winston up, in her arms, warmed him up, dashed home for crushed oyster shells and some other potions she thought would help. The sight of this proud creature, so diligent about guarding his hens, in this debilitated state was dispiriting.

On and on. The autumn was wet and misty, the winter cold and dank, and my chronic bronchitis came and stayed for weeks. A friend in California died. Paula's work kept her in New York much of the fall and early winter. Emma had a new job and could only drive up twice.

"You look funny," Anthony kept telling me.

My friend Becky and I had dinner together one night. "You look down," she said.

They were right.

I had put my protector to death, and now dark times had come. In the normal course of things, I have a lot of faith—not the official religious kind, but definitely a spiritual strain. I believe that if you do some good, don't quit, and keep trying, you will get somewhere. The idea has always sustained me, but that fall and winter, it seemed to melt away.

I didn't think I would ever live free of pain again, so I didn't think I'd be able to stay on the farm for long. I began imagining where all the animals should go if I had to leave. Rose and the donkeys and a few sheep would go live with Annie, I decided. Annie loved all animals and was crazy about Rose—not the most lovable of dogs, given her preference for work over almost anything.

And the donkeys would get homemade apple cookies, the kind she brought with her when she visited. Cuddling and cookies go a long way toward making a donkey happy.

The adaptable Clem, I decided, could live with Paula. The hens and Winston, if he survived, could return to the friend who'd given them to me, and I knew a farmer who would take the bulk of the sheep.

I doubted Paula would keep Bedlam Farm or that Emma would want to be there much, so I hoped somebody nice would buy it.

When I told Paula of this plan, so that it could be carried out "if anything happened," she was alarmed, then exasperated. She pointed out that I was improving, and that the physical therapy I'd started would likely bring further improvement. "I'm worried about you," she said. "You're depressed and you're getting alarmingly morbid. You're struggling with losing Orson, but you're not really dealing with it."

Everybody was telling me that—I was depressed and repressed, shutting down my emotions. I wished I knew how to respond differently, but I really didn't.

I *was* feeling morbid, though. I felt my time in this world was growing short. I kept telling people my plans and wishes for when I was gone. "Dad," Emma asked one night, "why are you talking like you're about to die?"

Not long after returning to the farm from the hospital, I found a message on my answering machine from Pam Leslie, the breeder who'd sold me Clementine.

"Are you calling to sell me Pearl?" I asked when I called Pam back, a running joke.

Pearl was never for sale. "You will have to pry her from my dead fingers," Pam always retorted. Pearl was a yellow Labrador, a two-time national champion, with the deepest, most mournful eyes I'd ever seen on a dog; she'd captured my heart from the first time I saw her at Pam's kennel. I called her the Sad-eyed Lady of the Lowlands, after the Bob Dylan song, and when I visited her in the kennel, I often sang her verses of the song in an appropriately nasal voice. Pearl loved it. When she came out of the kennel, she melted into my arms and gave me soft licks on the nose.

But she was a cornerstone of Pam's breeding program. "I've got a lot of money in that dog" was Pam's usual response. She'd spent thousands of dollars developing the line, and hoped for many litters of little Pearls.

So I wasn't surprised when Pam told me, "Forget it. Pearl isn't going anywhere."

But she asked if I might be in the mood to come by and visit. She had a black Lab for whom she wanted to find a home, so he could be socialized, exercised, and, from time to time, bred. "You and your farm would be great for him," Pam said. She wanted a joint arrangement, so that he'd have a home but wouldn't be neutered, and would be available for breeding.

Getting a dog, any dog, from Pam was not simple. She had a great passion for Labs, but also a long list of concerns and worries about where her dogs were going and how they'd fare. Matching dogs and people was a major priority.

She didn't particularly like Labs living with border collies (they ran too fast); she wasn't sure about a farm (a chance to pick up parasites); she didn't want the dogs overtrained or undertrained or not trained at all. She threw up a raft of roadblocks and reservations. The people who got one of her dogs were those who battled through them. Getting Clem had taken nearly a year of cajoling and convincing, and then waiting.

Pam did not know of Orson's death, I assumed. I hadn't talked about it much, and she didn't mention it. I wasn't looking for another dog—unless it was sweet, loving Pearl, and I was never going to get her to budge on Pearl.

Pam knew, too, that I didn't like these joint ownership arrangements, having dogs on the farm that were not neutered or spayed. I like to own my dogs without strings attached, and although every good breeder disagrees, I think unneutered dogs often spark behavioral issues with other dogs and are more likely to cause trouble. But I almost always felt like driving out to see Pam and her beautiful dogs.

So I drove over to Pawlet, Vermont. Pam and her assistant, Heather Waite, were waiting for me. Pearl, I noticed, was in a crate in the waiting room where Pam met prospective dog buyers—and grilled them until they squirmed.

"Miss Pearl," I yelped. "My sad-eyed girl." Usually, she was in her residence in the rear. Let out of her crate, she walked over slowly, put her head on my knee, turned those heartbreaking brown eyes on me, and dissolved into a heap by my feet. I lowered myself carefully to the floor and hugged her.

Pearl was all sweetness; she loved and wanted to be loved. Those of us who cherish Labs understand that however profound they seem, there's not always much going on behind those soulful looks (sometimes it's hamburger they really love). But Pearl seemed to recognize my sorrow, and to empathize.

I was sure she was waiting for me, waiting to leave behind the world of dog shows and breeding and join a family—mine. It would not happen, not for years. But I couldn't blame Pam; Pearl was the kind of dog that *ought* to be bred; there should be others as beautiful and calm and affectionate.

As usual, Pam and Heather and I dog-talked—breeding, training, Labs—for about half an hour. Then Pam went out to get Stripe, the black Lab she wanted to show me.

He came roaring out into the waiting room, a big, brawny, powerful dog, full of enthusiasm. He bounded from one end of the room to another. I could see what a great working dog he could make, how he'd love to run alongside the ATV through the woods. He'd hardly break a sweat.

"He's great," I said as Stripe went sniffing from one of us to the other. "But I don't know if he's for me." I liked mellower dogs. Anyway, I really wasn't looking for a dog just now.

Pam nodded. "He may not be for you, but the shame of it

is, you would be great for him." She never pushed a dog on anyone, though. If it didn't take, it didn't.

So she led Stripe away. Heather, who'd also become a friend, winked at me. "What about our crippled dog?" she said, quietly, to Pam. "What about Pearl?" Pam looked away, as if she couldn't bear the idea.

I stared at Pam. "You would let me have Pearl? For real?" She was still lying at my feet, awaiting pats and scratches.

Pearl, it turned out, had damaged one of her legs in a kennel accident and had undergone three painful, complicated surgeries to repair the damage. Then she'd spent months in a crate recovering, as the doctor had prescribed.

Her movement had been restricted. Confinement to a crate. Walking only on a leash. No running or jumping. She needed a lot of rehab, from massage to slow hill climbing, and there was a good chance she'd need more surgery.

Poor Pearl had had a rough time, suffered much pain and discomfort. She had screws in her knees and nylon filaments replacing her ligaments. No wonder she was walking slowly.

"You can have Pearl," Pam said. There was no discussion, which meant that she'd made up her mind. I knew this was a huge blow. Pearl had piled up ribbons, certificates, awards.

She was not a dog Pam would give up willingly, to anybody. But Pam put her dogs' interests first. Pearl had endured enough, she said; she didn't want to put her through the added strain of breeding or showing.

Orson had been dead for little more than six weeks. Given my uncertain back, I hadn't really thought about whether there would be a next dog—or, if so, what kind. Mostly, I'd been mulling where my dogs would go when I keeled over in pain.

But I didn't fuss over this decision, or give Pam time to

change her mind. I adored Pearl, her beautiful face, her wonderful temperament. We could hobble around together, rehabbing each other. In seconds, I was writing a check, and then I grabbed Pearl and would have run out of the kennel, if I could run.

Pam was usually happy to see her dogs go to good homes, but giving up Pearl, I could see, was wrenching. She couldn't watch.

As we headed out the door, Pearl eagerly walking by my side, Pam called after me. "Take care of her. And sorry about your border collie."

Pearl wove herself into my life as seamlessly as any creature could have. She did need more surgery, and we both did go through some long and painful rehabilitation. Whenever we went to the vet, Pearl would head straight for the operating room, even if she just needed a rabies shot.

She came everywhere with me, on shopping trips, to readings and talks. Wherever we went, she'd find some sucker and, within seconds, be lying on her back getting her belly rubbed. She had fans and friends everywhere.

My dog life had quieted, even with this new addition.

Rose seemed calmer after Orson's death. She spent more time next to me in my office, or sitting quietly in the garden, sometimes playing with Clem, more often keeping an eye on the flock. She accepted Pearl without rancor or fuss.

And Pearl and Clem, who were aunt and niece, bonded instantly, gnawing happily on each other, playing tug of war. I called them the Love Sisters.

Almost anybody who knew me, from UPS drivers to

landscapers and friends, had learned to approach the front-yard gate warily, a legacy of Orson's ferocious hubbub. Suddenly, it was a different experience. Instead of Orson, the Love Sisters were waiting, wriggling and wagging for treats and hugs. The local garden center often invited both of them for the day, to sit in the doorway and greet customers. Friends like Annie and Nicole—two of Orson's former girlfriends—came by to cuddle the girls and to help with Pearl's rehab. Town highway workers stopped to give the Labs biscuits.

Pearl couldn't run much those first few months—even getting to her feet after a nap took some effort—so she curled up next to me while I worked. She had every reason to be grumpy and aloof, but instead she was affectionate, forgiving, and calm. At the vet's office, they called her Perfect Pearl.

Of course, I couldn't run around much, either. Sometimes, when we encountered the slowly recovering Winston on our walks, I wondered at the spectacle of the three of us, limping and lurching around the farm.

Pearl had lived in a kennel her whole life; she seemed to relish being part of a family. She was so gentle I could bring her anywhere; none of the other animals on the farm minded her presence. She accompanied me to the barn to see the chickens, sheep, or donkeys.

Clem showed her the dark side of Lab life, where to find the biggest piles of tasty donkey droppings, how to roll in decaying animal carcasses or—even better—drag them into the house.

She loved to come sheepherding with Rose and me. While Rose moved the sheep around, Pearl would sit beside me, her head swiveling as Rose raced up and down the meadow. I thought she seemed puzzled as to why any dog would race around like that. She preferred to spend herding time leaning against my leg and waiting for a belly rub, then go back indoors for a siesta.

Pearl had enormous presence and dignity, the bearing and focus of an experienced show dog. She generally left the hard running and grunt work to the other dogs.

She was as different from Orson as a dog could be. Her very simplicity was healing. She just wanted to love and be loved, and had no agenda beyond that. She needed virtually no training; caused no trouble; demanded no more attention than I wanted to give. She did want to be with me, and I accommodated her.

When I worked, she lay by my right side; when the winter approached, she lay as close to the woodstove as she could get. There were titanium screws and other hardware in her leg; I figured they probably got cold in the winter.

It felt from the first as if she had lived with me forever. I don't believe that dogs choose us, as you sometimes hear their besotted owners say. But I do think dogs and other animals enter our lives for a reason, and in some cases, if you're paying attention, you can figure out what the purpose might be.

Orson radically altered my life: He came at a pivotal time and provoked—with no conscious part in the process, I'm sure—a series of actions and reactions that caused me to change almost everything about the way I lived and worked and thought.

Pearl was a dog hungry to leave behind her successful but transient life as a show and breeding dog and find someone to attach to, I was sure. That the someone was also pain-riddled, crippled, and sadly bereft was probably coincidental. This was her work. Unlike Orson, she was neither dominant, territorial, nor unpredictable. If his spirit was fiercely protective and instinctual, hers was unfailingly soothing and agreeable. Affection was her calling.

You could not look at that dog's face and fail to smile, and between Orson's death and my physical troubles, I hadn't smiled much for a while.

I didn't know, when he arrived, how much I needed Orson, but I did know I needed Pearl. When I was sad or unhappy, I would sit on the floor and she'd come limping over and put her head on my shoulder, lick me once or twice on the chin, then collapse onto the floor herself for tummy rubs.

Her own rehab continued, painfully and slowly. I learned how to massage her legs and gave her medication, and we went to see the same holistic Vermont vet who'd done so much to calm Orson, for acupuncture and chiropractic. As the weeks passed, Pearl grew stronger, more supple, more active. She began chasing sticks a bit.

In fact, I started taking Pearl along to my own physical therapy appointments. Entering the small building, she went to patients, resting her head next to them. If they ignored her, she moved on.

One sixteen-year-old had suffered awful knee damage in an accident, and his rehab—as he laboriously pedaled a stationary bicycle—was painful even to watch. Pearl zeroed in on him instantly; I loved to see him smile at her approach. An elderly woman trying to manage advanced arthritis always stayed to cuddle Pearl while I went through my own exercises. Soon, patients were calling to see when Pearl was coming. The therapists made it clear that I was not to show up without her.

She and I hobbled into the deep winter together. And,

slowly, things did start to brighten. Anthony bought a house on a hilltop, began a crash program to rebuild it, and let me run a forklift now and then. (I only put one hole in a wall.)

Winston survived, thanks to Annie, who built him a low perch and rigged up a heat lamp for the coldest nights. His crow was markedly weaker, but it was wonderful to hear it.

My back improved. Pearl and I went to physical therapy twice a week, and the exercises, heat, and massage began to work some magic. By the time the snow came, I was walking better than I had in a couple of years. I still faced limitations on what I could do. But there were stretches of the day when I was not in pain, and that made life better. To my family's relief, I issued fewer instructions as to the postmortem fate of my animals.

Clem, sensing an opportunity, started sleeping at the foot of my bed—at least until I dozed off myself, at which point she was prone to seizing my pillow and stretching out luxuriously. We tussled over blankets and space, but I loved waking up to her slurps on my face. I visited Orson's grave almost every day, sometimes riding up on the ATV, sometimes walking up the pasture, now that I could. I said hello, briefly told him what was going on. It was a nice spot with a good view.

On a farm, the miraculous cycle of life and death, loss and rebirth, keeps pulling you along, even if you're not really in the mood to go. So, of course, do dogs.

The tenor of life with my dogs had changed dramatically. If I no longer had a dog who could transform my life, I also no longer had one who would burst through a glass window, or frighten or harm anyone. There was less tension in Bedlam, fewer shouts and corrections, less anxiety and vigilance.

My other dogs could not replace Orson, nor fill the void

he left, yet in a curious way his departure had given me the life with dogs I'd always dreamed of. Be careful what you wish for.

On a farm, there is no stasis, however. Nothing stays the same three days in a row. I noticed the first rat in the fall, a big fat thing cheekily walking right by the barn door. When I yelled at him, he didn't move. I tossed a rock; he still didn't scramble.

I put the word out, therefore, on the country bullshit grapevine. In West Hebron, all news was broadcast via the Bedlam Corners Variety Store. Soon enough, I got a call from a farmer who had a cat he wanted to get rid of.

I was never much drawn to cats, and even if I had been, Orson was not. They seemed to me slithery and remote. I didn't really get having an animal you couldn't herd sheep or take a walk with. What use were cats?

But the rats were invading, and so sizable that early on I mistook one for a rabbit. The farmers told me there was nothing much to be done: Rats, naturally drawn to farms, were smart, hardy, and tough to get rid of. There were countless holes in stone walls and rotted silos they could nest in. They figured out traps. And I couldn't spread poisons around a barnyard full of dogs, sheep, donkeys, and chickens.

The farmer who'd called was about to weed out his own posse and had one in mind for me, because she was accustomed to dogs. Young, scrawny, and mottled (cat lovers would call her a tortoiseshell), she got her name—Mother—from her habit of caring for kittens, whether they were hers or not.

Upstate, barn cats are mythic figures. Elusive and reclusive, they prowl barns and pastures, sleep in haylofts, wage war on rodents and snakes.

They die often—and frequently brutally—from disease, neglect, and abuse; from poison or stray dogs or attacks by predators like foxes and coyotes; from target practice by kids or hunters. They get hit by cars or, in the worst cases, waste away from starvation and exposure. When their numbers increase (few are spayed or neutered), they often are shot. Some of the softer farmers put heat lamps in their barns or let their barn cats into basements and mudrooms on sub-zero nights. Most don't.

Did I need a barn cat?

Rose ran the farm and didn't like cats either, though she was less adamant about that than Orson. But the rat population was booming. So, with many misgivings, I agreed to take Mother, and my neighbor drove her over in a cardboard box. I had the distinct feeling that if I hadn't taken her she wasn't headed for a shelter.

Mother was surprisingly friendly. She took to me right away. She loved to be stroked and scratched, and she purred when she saw me and curled around my legs. She was always ravenous and seemed astounded by the cans of cat food I ferried out to her in the barn. She was also instantly businesslike, scoping out the rats the second she arrived.

I took her to the vet and had her spayed and immunized, then put a collar on her, so strangers would know she wasn't a stray.

Rose was not hospitable. The minute Mother returned from the vet and entered the barnyard, Rose roared down the pasture hill to drive off this unimpressive-looking intruder.

It was one of Rose's rare errors in judgment. The cat sat

perfectly still until the charging border collie was about four inches away, then she calmly turned and raked the dog's nose with one sharp swipe of her paw. Rose, unlike Orson, was not one to make the same mistake twice. From that point on, even when Mother was right in front of her, Rose pretended not to notice.

Mother staked out the barn and the barnyard right away, sashaying back and forth at the gate, taunting the dogs, strutting her stuff, almost daring anybody to start something. Nobody did.

From Mother's first day, the rodent carcasses began piling up. She left the first right by my back door; it was enormous. Daily offerings followed. This caused accompanying minor problems when Clem and Pearl, wagging delightedly, began bringing the corpses into the house. But the pest population plummeted. I was impressed; this cat delivered.

Greeting Mother quickly became part of my morning routine. I left a bowl of dry kibble in an empty stable, but I also brought her a dish of canned cat food each day. Mother was always waiting for me, purring, meowing, circling. I put out a de-icer bucket so that she would always have water, even on bitter-cold nights. And I brought occasional snacks, table scraps, or a cup of warm milk. As with dogs and donkeys, food went a long way toward establishing a good relationship.

Mother seemed quite content in the barn. Unlike a dog, she had no need for or interest in sharing my life. Yet we had a real understanding, a lot of mutual affection.

As winter approached, I worried about the cold—I'd always heard that cats hated the cold—even though Mother was filling out and growing a thicker coat. With a friend's help, I made her a sort of igloo in the barn loft, a cozy construction of hay bales with a fuzzy blanket underneath.

I sometimes wondered, as the temperatures dropped, whether I should let Mother into the house. Every dog I've ever had would have happily come inside. But Mother didn't seem to care. She was happy in her space and happy to leave me in mine. She was willing to accept occasional gifts, but she didn't need my charity.

Every now and then she disappeared for a day or two, and I went out to the barn, anxiously calling her name. You could not, I realized, have it both ways. A barn cat was not really a pet. In the tradition of barn cats, Mother eventually reappeared, and no one knew where she'd been or why.

But the rats—at least the live ones—disappeared.

Once in a while, when I took out the garbage or left the dogs behind to stroll under a full moon, Mother appeared at my side and strolled along with me. "Hey, Mother," I said. She rarely met my gaze, but she walked along with her tail up, her eyes sweeping the darkness. I was happy to have her company.

There was life after death, it seemed. Pearl was a different kind of dog from Orson, and Mother a different kind of animal altogether.

They bolstered me, Pearl with her inexhaustible affection, Mother with her novelty, a new kind of connection to the animal world.

In retrospect, their animal natures marked the end of that darker time; they brought their own brands of comfort. If they could not replace Orson, they did show me that Orson was not the only animal that could take me outside myself.

Around that time, a message turned up on my answering machine from Lesley, the shaman. She wanted to come talk to me.

CHAPTER THIRTEEN

Home to the Dog Star

Conventional wisdom holds that the older people get, the more sagacious they become. This has not been my experience. The older I get, the less I think I know, the less certainty I have, the more I realize how much we don't know and will never understand.

My friend Anthony, young and filled with energy, is drawn to detailed plans; if they're good plans—his often are—they will work, he thinks.

I'm convinced most plans are doomed, hubristic notions just waiting to unravel. Orson is the classic example, the product of my plans that failed and failed and failed.

Yet his good works on my behalf transcend death. It took me some time to see it, but I know that he'll always be taking care of me, in one sense or another, whether he's with me or not.

Orson reenergized my work. He reconnected me to nature, brought me to the farm, introduced me to the pleasure of other animals, led me to true friends, cracked open my consciousness, deepened my spirituality and sense of possibility. Three years ago I would have no more been yakking on the phone with a shaman than I would be playing in the NFL.

Nor would I have grasped the concept of an animal's spirit guiding and helping me, something I now see and feel almost daily.

Orson helped me, deep into my sixth decade, to stay open, to not shut down. In many ways, that may turn out to be his greatest gift.

I'm not a shaman and I don't wish to be; I don't have those special qualities. But I love the stories people like Lesley bring back from some other world. I can't say if these stories are true. I don't measure Lesley's every word against the literal facts; to do that is to miss the point, to blind oneself to the possibility of a greater truth. Reality is not about how Lesley learns something and when she learned it, it's about her ability to sense what an animal might feel or know, and to translate that for people like me.

I no longer doubt that there are people with gifts I don't have, who know things I don't know. Lesley is one of those. After Orson's death, Lesley took a number of "journeys" with Orson; some I requested, some occurred spontaneously.

What she learned and experienced was mesmerizing. More than anything else, I found her reports profoundly healing.

I learned early in life that it's dangerous to show emotion, so I generally don't; maybe I never will. Lesley understood that that didn't mean I couldn't feel. She saw the broken parts of me, just as she saw the broken parts of Orson. She saw what we meant to each other, how those broken parts fit together like pieces of a puzzle. She helped me to come to terms with what had happened when I couldn't do it by myself.

Lesley had visited the farm; she'd met Orson. She knew he had problems; she knew he'd attacked and bitten several people. When we met, she hadn't read any of my books; we hadn't talked much about my life or my past. Yet in a short time, she had come to know me well, to understand my concerns and choices. I trusted her, something that doesn't come easily to me.

She called herself a shaman but I thought of Lesley as an intuitive. She grasped the spirit and sense of animals—and people—better than almost anyone I'd met.

In the days before Orson's death, I had talked to almost no one but Paula and Anthony about what I was thinking, what I had decided to do. Yet Lesley had picked up on it.

I'll pass along what she told me. I relate the story faithfully, but I can't say whether or not it's true. You'll have to decide that for yourself, and make of it what you will.

She had successfully encountered Orson in a journey, Lesley said when I called. When she received messages from animals, she explained, she usually saw them sitting at the edge of a lake; if they wished to communicate with her, they would show her images they wanted her to see. Sometimes they chose not to.

"I had a strange visit with Orson," she said. "The message I got was that he was released, that he was happy and free."

Released from what? I asked, taken aback.

"From being Orson," she said. "But he is worried about you. It was strange, I don't really know what to make of it. He wanted to tell me that he was still taking care of you, watching over you. I don't know what this means."

I told her that Orson was dead and why. And I asked her to journey to see him again.

Lesley came to the farm a few weeks later, and we sat in the living room, warming ourselves with a blaze in the woodstove and mugs of hot tea.

My old barns loomed in their reddish, aging glory through the tall windows. The sun was fading, vanishing behind the hill. Rose never stuck around when company came, but this time she lay at Lesley's feet, not budging. Usually so restless and busy, she behaved as if she wanted to hear every word. Clem was dozing nearby, Pearl leaning against Lesley's leg, getting her neck scratched.

She had met Orson again, Lesley said. He was sitting by the lake at first, but he was waiting for her, eager to show her another place: some dark woods up in the hills way above the farmhouse. There was darkness, then light; dense groves of trees, then brightness. I recognized this description as the woods through which Orson and I often rode on the ATV to meet Sirius, the Dog Star.

This, Lesley explained, was Orson's new home, where his spirit lived. He remained powerfully connected to me, she said, but he'd known it was time to go, and he'd been ready to go. He was remaining behind, she said, to fulfill the terms of our contract, to meet his obligations, as he believed I had tried to meet mine.

This was startling. Lesley didn't know of our trips to see the Dog Star, and I'd certainly not used the word "contract" to describe the understanding I thought Orson and I had.

Why was Orson staying behind? I asked.

To help me finish my project, my new book.

Even more unsettling. Lesley didn't know I was trying to write about my life with Orson. I told her about it, about what I'd learned about the Dog Star and the dog days.

Orson, she said, did not stay near his grave site, and now she understood why. His home was up in the woods, under the Dog Star.

It made me unreasonably happy to think his spirit might still hover nearby.

Would he stay here always? I asked.

No, she said. Only until I was finished with the book; then he would move on. I could always connect with him there in the woods, but he would leave the farm, leave me.

Did he ever come closer?

Yes, Lesley said. Whenever I was writing, he was there with me, resting his head on my right foot.

My heartbeat quickened. In recent weeks, I'd often felt pressure on my right foot when I was working; in fact, I kept telling Pearl and Clem to get off, until I looked down and saw they weren't there. I figured it might be a neurological symptom. It wasn't painful, particularly, just the sense of a weight. Paula thought I should mention it to the spinal surgeon when I next saw him in New York.

We talked for a while about Orson, about this revelation that made no sense and, simultaneously, plenty of sense. Lesley said Orson was "stressed, exhausted, spent" by the pressure and stimulation of his troubled life in the human world. Sometimes, his brain felt overloaded; his head almost burned, it was so filled with sights and sounds and failures and responsibilities.

But when she'd seen him, she said, he was at peace.

I was struck by the feeling in the room. A few friends had come by—Anthony and two of Orson's girlfriends, Nicole and Annie—and I'd invited them to join us. Normally I cherish my privacy, but these people had shared my life and Orson's, and it seemed natural for them to be there and hear what Lesley had learned.

Much more than me, they instinctively embraced the idea of a shaman, had no doubts or distance from it. There was no tension in the room, no hostility, anger, or regret. It was a serene gathering. Anthony, who left to go to work, said he felt it, too. In both our lives, gatherings of people were not always tranquil. But there was great trust in this room, complete safety.

Still, sorrow engulfed me. I felt at that moment that humans—our demands and expectations, certainly including my own—had failed this creature at every point. And had eventually killed him, even though he'd been of as great service to a human as any dog has.

As Lesley told about Orson, still present up in the woods, lying on my right foot while I worked, fulfilling his contract to me, then ready to move on, I saw that Nicole and Annie were crying. I felt selfish. I had forgotten how many other people loved this dog.

I wasn't crying, though. Orson's death seemed terribly sad to me, but Lesley's story didn't. Orson was released, free, at peace. Yet he was still watching over me, for a little while longer at least.

What had happened to make him behave so uncharacteristically? I asked her. Why would he attack those people?

Lesley wasn't sure. She believed that perhaps his recent troubles had given me a reason to relinquish him, a way for him to leave. This wasn't a conscious or deliberate plan, she said, or an idea he could put into words. Our connection was powerful, she said, timeless. But animals often find a way of getting humans to let go when it's time. He had simply had enough.

Word of this gathering spread through my hamlet, and I expected raised eyebrows and ridicule, of the kind I would probably have offered myself, a few months earlier. The news didn't generate scoffing, however, but great interest. Every other day, it seemed, women—and some men—were dropping off pictures of dogs, cats, goats, and horses they hoped Lesley could journey to and communicate with. I put a bowl near the front door to store the growing pile of envelopes.

It began to feel perfectly normal—like driving over to get the paper or pick up groceries—to collect these pictures, write names and questions on the back, and send them to a friendly vet in Vermont, where Lesley would pick them up, read them, and then, when she was able, encounter this array of creatures.

We had a regular shamanic communications network going, all sorts of animals getting visits and relaying messages. We all followed one another's questions, waited for the shaman's answers, discussed the implications. Actually, it was great.

It was enthralling to think that Orson was resting on my foot, was feeling free and happy. To picture his presence up beneath the Dog Star gave me quiet joy.

Even my grumpy old neighbor Carr, a farmer who has mocked me at every turn for the money I spend on vet care, the price I pay for my purebred dogs, and for even letting a shaman set foot on my property, heard of our shamanic communiqués and came by with a picture of his ancient German shepherd Betsy, a veteran, battle-scarred farm dog he adored.

Usually full of opinions and well-meaning suggestions about how to run my farm, Carr was quiet that morning. "She's got some tumor or something, the vet says," he told me, looking toward the ground. Betsy had always gone with him everywhere. "I hate to ask, and I wouldn't blame you if you told me to go to hell, but maybe you could send this picture along to that friend of yours. Maybe she could let me know how Betsy's really feeling, so I can make whatever decisions I gotta make."

I nodded and patted Carr on the back. Nobody has a more difficult, or more loving, view of animals than a farmer. I told him I was sure Lesley would do her best and would call him. He never mentioned the encounter to me again, but a few weeks later, he took Betsy to the vet and put her down.

It occurred to me as I wrote this concluding chapter that if Lesley's understanding of Orson's spirit was correct, then he intended to leave me, and Bedlam Farm, once I finished. That gave me pause. Probably I should have thought of it sooner, but I hadn't. The last word of the last chapter would be our final farewell.

I dreaded it.

I had tucked the ATV into one of the barns for the winter—a thick layer of snow and ice coated the ground—but when I pulled off the plastic cover and turned the key, it started right up.

I swathed myself in scarves and hoods and thick gloves and rode up the hill. The ATV chugged through the snow easily, and I cut through the pasture, across the top of the hill, and into the woods.

This was tougher going, but the ATV plowed through. There was too much snow to risk pulling off the trail, so I turned the machine off and went on through the trees on foot. I wished I had brought Rose or Clem. I hadn't thought to bring a cell phone. But I did not feel alone.

I walked the hundred or so yards into the woods and found, poking up through the snow, the rock where Orson and I sat on those misty dog day mornings. Up here I had no trouble showing emotions.

It was bitter and the sun was sinking quickly. I couldn't stay long.

So this was it, then, the end of our journey together, our tale of friendship and faithfulness.

You gave me so much, I thought, and I gave you so little back. In one sense, isn't that the story of humans and dogs?

Still, this should by rights be a happy story, not a sad one. His was a life to celebrate. Orson was a good dog; he'd served me well. I had done the best I could for him, too. That it was not enough is the stuff of life itself. We can only try. We can feel certain of little.

I closed my eyes and tried to journey to Orson, as Lesley had. I tried to picture him resting by a lake, to feel his spirit. Nothing. I don't have that gift.

But I have others. I am a writer; I can tell stories. If I couldn't see Orson, receive messages from him, then I could imagine him. If I couldn't summon him, then I could make him up; that was *my* power, my own gift. I had been doing that all my life.

So, since it would not come to me magically, I invented a final encounter with my dog, a way of staying with him a bit longer.

My story, the one I made up:

The woods are beautiful, bright and sunlit. I hear a flurry, light footsteps approaching in the snow.

Orson comes out of the shadows to me, right over to the

rock. He's even more beautiful than I remember, so regal and proud, ears up, eyes wide.

He doesn't throw himself at me, shower me with licks, jump into my lap. He simply comes close, comfortable with himself, finally able, I imagine, to be free of commands and demands, to do as he wants, not what people keep yelling at him to do. He is free to be the powerful, loving, intelligent, and instinctive creature he was born to be.

Though I can see he's very pleased to see me, he doesn't spin around or paw at me for pats. That frantic, aroused quality is gone; he is quiet, different.

I stroke his glossy coat and after a bit, he does nuzzle me, leans his head against my chest. "Nice place, your new home," I say.

We sit quietly together for a few minutes. He is available if I want to find him, he will come if I need him. He's going away, but not leaving me in the sense I fear. None of this is spoken, just understood, and once I grasp that, we seem to be done.

I don't know if there's a spirit world or if Orson inhabits it. I hope so, because that sounds like a better world for him than ours. But even in my own story, I can't know.

But because this is my own story, I hug him one last time. Lesley is right: our closeness is beyond words, beyond consciousness, unbreakable.

I walked back through the woods to the ATV and rode slowly back down the trail, across the pasture, past his grave, back down to the house.

The Love Sisters were the first to come bounding out the

door, tails wagging, thrilled to see me. Rose followed, in a bouncy mood, licking my hand.

It's okay, she seemed to be saying. We are not him, but we are here and we love you too. Or perhaps that's just what I hoped she felt.

It seemed as if I had been gone a long time. I dropped to the ground, hugged all my dogs, and then got up, brushed myself off, took off my boots. I made myself a cup of tea and headed back into my office.

It was nearly dark now. The sheep were beginning their long nightly trek to the top of the hill, where they would cluster and spend the night. The donkeys were in the pole barn; to my dismay, they'd developed a habit of gnawing on the wooden ladder to the hayloft. Winston was leading the hens into the barn, to their perches. I glimpsed Mother peeking out the barn door, about to begin her murderous night patrols.

I poked the fire in the woodstove and turned on the computer. Clem had settled on the sofa with her favorite plush pheasant, which would soon be shredded to bits. Pearl lay down next to me, and Rose darted into the crate next to my desk.

I don't know if I imagined it, if I was still half inside my story, but I felt a twinge, pressure on my right foot. It could have been any of the dogs. It could have been my disintegrating spine. It could have been nothing. I didn't look.

So this was it, the last turn in the life of a good dog.

Good-bye, friend, and safe travels home.

From top: Rose, Clem, and Pearl

Owning and loving a dog is a very individual experience. Orson's story was complex, his behavioral problems probably stemming from multiple sources.

Some factors—his litter, his early training and socialization, genetics—predate his joining my household. The environment I provided, my own training attempts, my personality may also have had an impact.

My choice for Orson was only that: my choice for my dog. Animal lovers have strong opinions on such issues; some will likely condemn my decision.

I believe this kind of choice is intensely personal; there are simply no universal rules. When all is said and done, we are, each of us, on our own.

If your dog shows behavioral problems, such as arousal or aggression, please consult a vet, trainer, or veterinary behaviorist. Many dogs can be successfully retrained, reoriented, or re-homed. I selected a particular option; there are others.

Please also remember, however, that millions of Americans—many of them children—are bitten by dogs each year, some very seriously. This is a moral issue relating to people and dogs that, sadly, many of us who love dogs may have to address.

It didn't take long for the angry comments to start piling up at the online booksellers. "*A Good Dog:* Bad Owner," blared the headline on one review. Another declared, "Bad Book. Bad Author. Bad Man."

At the same time, as my book tour took me around the country, I was spending almost every night in one bookstore or another, awaiting similar assaults—and not getting any. "I've been there," an elderly woman declared at my first reading in nearby Cambridge, New York, giving me a big hug and pressing a tattered picture of her late dog into my hands. It was going to be that kind of a book, I told myself.

I'd expected mixed feelings about *A Good Dog* and my decision to put Orson down. And I was right.

"How dare you kill Orson and exploit him by writing a book about it?" a reader in Miami demanded via e-mail. "How could you kill this dog?" scolded another. "Shame on you. My dog bit three people and I have him confined safely in a double chain-link fence in the backyard where he is not allowed near any humans other than me. Why didn't you do that?" Some people thought I'd given up on Orson without trying the simplest remedies. I should have called Cesar, one anguished dog lover on a border collie mailing list insisted—

referring to the famous (and much better-selling) trainer and author. Surely Cesar would have helped. It was striking how often people used the word "just," as if there were simple options for Orson they didn't seem to think had occurred to me. "Why didn't he just put a BEWARE OF DOG sign up in his yard?" wrote one critic. Correspondents expressed outrage that I didn't "just muzzle him" or "just tie him up in the yard" or "just build a higher fence." A professor wrote to say that he was withholding judgment until I considered this question: Should dogs be held to human standards of acceptable behavior and safety? I answered that I wasn't really awaiting his judgment but, instead, was living with mine.

It's a healthy thing, I believe—especially for writers, who work alone and only intermittently face their readers—to have these exchanges, even if they sometimes grow testy. The challenges went back and forth in cyberspace at least twenty times a day for months, and they'll continue for many months more. It's the public's right to grill me, my obligation to try to respond.

Having written online for years, I know the importance of reacting to angry e-mail with patience and calm. So often, people hit the "send" button impulsively, emotionally. They later confess that they never thought their messages would be read, let alone answered.

To me, this phenomenon of online hostility is a potent metaphor for the disconnection so many in our society feel, hurling accusations and complaints, certain that no one will pay the slightest attention. Trying to overcome that feeling is important, part of a writer's task. So I do pay attention, and once personal contact is established, real communication often becomes possible. "I'm sorry for my tone," one reader e-mailed me a few days after she'd fired off a shocked and angry blast and I'd replied. "I know you loved Orson and I really have no right to judge you. I'm sorry for your loss." When I got discouraged, or felt misunderstood, I went outside with Rose and took the sheep to graze in the meadow, or puttered along on the ATV with my newest adoptee, Izzy, or lay on the floor and cuddled with Pearl. My beautiful, happy, and loving dogs did their work. They were a powerful antidote, both to Orson's loss and to the irate questions about his death.

I've believed for some time that I never really know what my books are about until people read them and tell me. Books are rarely only about the subjects I think they're about.

This one, I gather, was partly about life with a dog I loved but also about loss, something we'll all face, if we haven't already. The book also, it turned out, provoked some fundamental questions about dogs and humans. How much do we love our dogs? Can we sometimes love them too much?

Where are the boundaries shaping what a human being can and ought to do for an animal? Are we coming to love and value dogs more than humans?

Happily, I had face-to-face encounters with dog lovers where we mulled such questions together. Lengthy book tours are grueling, even disorienting, but they also give me a chance to have rolling conversations with dog people from one end of the country to the other. The tour for *A Good Dog* took up much of the fall, beginning in New York state, drifting into New England and down into the Mid-Atlantic, then through the Midwest to the mountain states and the Pacific Northwest.

At the start, almost no one had yet read the book, so I was

peppered with questions about Orson—whose story people had followed for several years—and how he was doing. "Uh-oh," said a woman in Washington, suddenly anxious. "From the way you're talking, I don't think this book ends so happily." No, I acknowledged with a sad smile; it doesn't.

I didn't want to spoil the experience of reading the book, but I didn't want to misrepresent it, either. Many dog lovers, I know, simply can't bear to read accounts of a dog's death. Others just like to be forewarned.

As the tour progressed, and more and more people showed up who had read the book, the tenor of the gatherings changed. The crowds were quieter, sweeter, distinctly understanding, and sympathetic.

We didn't dwell too much on sorrow. I told funny stories about Orson, and anecdotes about the movie HBO Films was making of *A Dog Year,* the book that introduced him. It was lovely to hear laughter on this book tour.

My overwhelming sense of the dog world is that for all our excesses, our sometimes unbounded immersion in our dogs— readers showed me countless snapshots of their dogs; they also shared cell-phone videos, poetry, songs, and sketches—this is a loving bunch. People waiting in line shed many tears for past dogs, dead dogs, and living dogs who pierced the heart. Dog people are generous souls, and their affection enveloped me. It's along the coasts, it seems to me, that dog love is the most intense—almost as if the most urbanized and suburbanized Americans grow so harried, so disconnected from one another, that they sometimes invest dogs with extraordinary emotional and cognitive qualities. Midwesterners like to portray themselves as more grounded and down-to-earth, and I'm starting to think they could be right. Surely they love their pets, but they seem to have less need to turn animals into little people, and more capacity to enjoy them for what they are. Perhaps people there aren't so many years removed from farm life, so there's more familiarity with animals, more understanding of their unpredictable natures, less tendency to make them emotional surrogates. On the other hand, a formidable older woman named Sadie waited half an hour to get a book signed at the Annie Bloom Bookshop in a beautiful neighborhood of Portland, Oregon. When she finally made her way to the front of the line, she planted a big kiss on my cheek. "I love your books, Jon," she announced. "You are by no means perfect, but you are trying. I appreciate that." I didn't encounter a single hostile person or comment in the nearly two months of the tour.

Online, it's a different story. Much of the e-mail has been empathetic and supportive, or gently disapproving. People send me stories (and photos) of their own lifetime dogs, dogs they loved and lost, dogs they lived happily with, troubled dogs who lost their lives or had to be put down. But the denunciations weren't long in coming, and they've never really stopped.

It's been a powerful, if sometimes truncated conversation, and it teaches me things I need to know, brings me stories I want to hear.

Some readers seemed to be expecting more of a Disney story, a yarn about a beguiling rascal who drove his bumbling owner nuts—and yet somehow, everything worked out. Some expected—demanded—a happy ending. They didn't anticipate that the rascal would turn aggressive and that no, it didn't all work out. I was sorry to upset and disappoint them.

"You didn't love Orson more than I did," I wrote one stricken woman who'd accused me of "murdering" my dog. She apologized. Sometimes, it felt almost as if people were appropriating Orson's death, making my loss theirs. Some of my concerns about people, love, animals, and humanity seemed confirmed by their anguish and fury. In my replies, I often asked my correspondents to be careful, to make sure that their love for their dogs didn't overwhelm their humility and humanity. Weren't most of us doing the best we could under the circumstances we faced?

Tellingly, in the thousands of questions I received after the book's publication, by e-mail and in person, nobody ever asked me about the people that Orson bit. It was striking how much feeling people had for my dog and how little concern for the humans in this tale. They've become the story's invisible characters.

They haunted me, then and now. The young boy Orson attacked, tearing his sweatshirt, was uninjured but remains a bit fearful of dogs. I've arranged for him to visit with Pearl, Clementine, and Izzy, though, and they are hard to resist. He is beginning to trust dogs again.

The young woman in the garden still carries a scar, but she's careful never to blame Orson for the attack. "He didn't mean any harm," she says, loyal to him still. Her affection speaks to the ambiguity of this creature, who could embody so much love and so much confusion. As for my neighbor, I've not seen him much, but he's not the type to worry about a dog bite.

It's a measure of Orson's potent personality that so many people who'd never seen or met him were enraged at his death. And it was predictable. How could I write about this lovable and engaging creature and not expect people to be shocked and upset to learn of his death, not at the hands of a stranger, a drunk driver, or a terminal disease, but at my own.

I came to understand that I'd veered from the expected

script. My dog story wasn't supposed to end this way. "It is not *Marley & Me*," one livid reviewer charged, and he was right.

"How dare you write a book and kill a dog," wrote an aspiring writer with two rescue border collies. "That is not the story I bought, not the book I expected to read. I want my money back."

But my story was Orson's life and death. I could write only about what had happened, not what other people wish had happened, or what might happen to them. If she really wanted her money back, I responded to the writer, she could send me her address and I would mail her a refund. Then she could patronize another writer, one who would always meet her expectations, always do what she thought best. But of course, I never heard from her again.

A Good Dog has been my most successful book by far. It got warm and appreciative reviews. The tour I'd dreaded proved healing and rewarding. People were surprised, saddened, and sometimes critical, but I also found a river of good faith, an awareness that I loved this dog and appreciated him, and that I didn't make any such decision lightly, without exploring and pondering the options. I've found the response to the book more affirming than not. I feel secure, if not happy, with my actions. What I did was best for me and, I believe, best for him.

One way or another, I visit Orson's grave just about every day. Sometimes I herd the sheep along the crest of the hill where he is buried. Sometimes the dogs and I motor by on the ATV, pausing long enough for me to yell "Yo!" or "How's it going?"

Lesley the shaman tells me, however, that Orson is

nowhere near the grave. He left the farm after I finished writing *A Good Dog,* she says, but comes back periodically to check on me and the farm. When he does, he usually visits the spot in the woods—about a mile from his tombstone—where we used to gaze up at Sirius the Dog Star together. If I want to, I can always find him there, she says. But I haven't gone back to that clearing for months. I couldn't summon his spirit the last, and only, time I tried. Maybe I'm not ready to see him again. Maybe I don't really believe he's there. Maybe it's too painful either way.

But I think I may ask Lesley to take one of her journeys and report back on what she learns. And when the snow clears, I think I'll take the ATV and motor up into the woods. If we meet, Orson and I, we will look each other in the eye, neither of us having any reason to look away. It's my belief that we kept faith with each other, that we did right by each other, that we honored the ancient contract between dog and man.

I'll always love this dog, always miss him, and I hope I'll always also see him as the conflicted and troubled animal he was. There's no shame there, for either of us.

For me, dogs have always been a measure of our humanity, not only in how we regard and treat them, but perhaps, even more important, in how they help us to regard and treat our fellow humans. The miracle of dogs for me—and Orson was the living embodiment of this—is the way they brought me back to people. Orson helped fill my life with friends, perhaps his greatest gift to me. I loved him, I love them. Through him, I came to see that the work of dogs is not to lead us away from humanity but toward it.

So many people seem sure about what ought to be done about dogs—theirs or mine. Orson taught me not that I always know what should happen, but that I don't. We are alone at times like this, confined by our own sensibility, ethics, and experiences. Big decisions are often lonely ones.

Among other things, Orson taught me that I know little. I can only hope, in my remaining time, that I will continue trying to learn, to work on improving myself and on loving and caring for people as much as—perhaps more than—my dogs.

So I thank all the many people who contacted me, no matter what they said. It was good of them to respond so strongly to my work that they wanted to get in touch.

I knew I wouldn't please everyone, nor was I much inclined to try. I'm comfortable with my decision. It was, for me and my dog, the best we could reach under the circumstances we faced. Now, I'll focus on other dogs and other questions. I won't ever forget Orson, and I hope I'll never stop reaping and absorbing the many gifts and lessons he brought me. But life with dogs, and life on my farm, shows me daily that life goes on. One way or another, Orson and I have gone on with it.

Hebron, N.Y.
December 2006

ACKNOWLEDGMENTS

Thanks to my editor, Bruce Tracy, for insisting that I had to tell Orson's story, and for guiding me so carefully and sympathetically through its writing.

Thanks to Richard Abate for fighting hard for me. I thank Dennis Ambrose and Ed Cohen for their careful copyediting and proofreading of my work.

I don't really know how to appropriately thank the usual suspects: my wife, Paula Span, who has hung on to what she's taken to calling "the runaway train that is Katz," and my daughter, Emma Span, for her love, humor, decency, and great mind.

I thank Anthony Armstrong for giving me the gift of real friendship, even in middle age, when I had begun to despair of finding it, and for his hard work and artistry in restoring Bedlam Farm. His wife, Holly Beth, and daughter, Ida Jane, have provided me with love, support, and good times.

I appreciate Peter Hanks for his photographic vision, which has helped bring my work to life, and for selling me Elvis, my Brown Swiss steer. Thanks also to Jane, Robin, and Dean Hanks for their support and encouragement since I landed in the country.

I am grateful for the friendship of Becky MacLachlan;

Meg, Rob, Hunter, and Elizabeth Southerland; and Bill and Maria Heinrich. I am grateful to Jesse and Ralph Corey.

Life on Bedlam Farm would not be possible without my friend and helper Annie DiLeo, the Goat Lady of Cossayuna.

I am fortunate to have the friendship and wisdom of Lesley Nase, who has opened my heart and mind to the spiritual world of animals.

Thanks, too, to Stanley Mickiewicz for his help and fine woodwork; to Ginny Tremblay, for first showing me Bedlam Farm and being so good a friend; to Alice and Harvey Hahn for helping care for this great old farmhouse; to Pat Freund for introducing me to the wonderful world of donkeys; to Nancy Higby and her Dirt Divas for restoring the gardens of Bedlam Farm. Two great dog breeders, Deanna Veselka of Wildblue Border Collies, and Pam Leslie and Heather Waite of Hillside Labradors, are responsible for the wonderful dogs who have so shaped my life.

Thanks to the veterinarians of Borador Animal Hospital and the Granville Small Animal Veterinary Service, especially Mary Menard, Whitney Pressler, and Jeff Meyers. And to Stephanie Mills-Holtzman. And to the Granville Large Animal Service.

I am grateful to Dr. Bernard Rawlins and Dr. Dan Richman of the New York Hospital for Special Surgery, and to Kathy Metzger of the Vermont Sports Medicine Center, for helping me move again.

Thanks to John Sweenor for teaching me the beauty of ATVs, American cars, and aggressive tires.

And, of course, I won't ever be able to really express my gratitude to Orson, the dog who launched me on this great journey, a debt I could never repay.

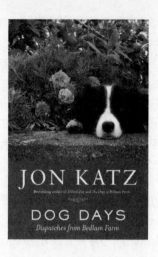

Here's a preview of Jon Katz's new book, *Dog Days*:

AT FIRST I JUST LISTENED TO THE PHONE MESSAGE A COUPLE OF times. I wasn't sure I should call back.

I'm fond of Amy, a rescue person, but she also makes me a bit nervous. I'm wary of the emotional intensity surrounding animal rescue and some of the people who do it.

Amy regularly calls my farm, and others, seeking homes for animals in trouble. They might be donkeys retiring from duty in national parks, abused goats from Buffalo, cats, rabbits, and dogs, of course.

Sometimes—I've told Amy this—I worry that the desire to rescue can become an unceasing cycle. There's no end to the need. If you love animals—any animals—you will sooner or later become acquainted with their suffering. Amy's small farm along the Vermont border is already crammed with animal refugees she's taken in.

I think what makes me uncomfortable is that under different circumstances, I could probably become Amy. Or my sister, who shares a small house and yard some hours west of here with rescue dogs (eight ailing Newfoundlands with heart disease, at this juncture, plus some dogs in foster care), donkeys, ducks, goats, a horse, chickens—the cast of characters changes often.

I don't want the rescue impulse to dominate or overwhelm me; it could, I know, swallow me up. Yet I am drawn to it. So Amy understands, when she leaves messages, that sometimes I return the calls, sometimes I don't. I understand why she keeps trying: She sees my place as a beautiful haven that could shelter a lot of animals in trouble. But while I've helped Amy place donkeys, dogs, and horses, she hasn't placed any with me.

Still, rescue people are often determined advocates who fight hard. When an animal and a human connect, when the match feels perfect, they like to say the dog or cat or horse has "hit the jackpot." It's pure joy for them to see, the thing they most aspire to. So Amy had learned to be wily.

"Hey, Jon, this is Amy," said the message that arrived late on a dark March afternoon. "Listen, I have a couple of donkeys from the U.S. Bureau of Land Management out west who need homes." (They take tourists on rides up difficult trails.) "I know you have donkeys. Could you take one? Probably not, but I thought I'd take a shot.

"Oh, and also," she added, almost as an afterthought, "we found some border collie puppies on a farm nearby. The owner's been sick and hasn't been on the farm in ages, maybe a couple of years. A nice caretaker feeds the dogs, but they spend most of their lives in a little outbuilding behind a fence and they're alone most of the time. And now the farm is for sale, so they need homes.

"And there's this older border collie—about three, I think—who's the father. Quite a character. He's not housebroken. I don't think he's ever lived in a house or been around people much, just the caretaker. He's been fed and cared for, but never trained or given any kind of work. Flo's seen the dogs; she knows them. Call me if you can help."

I saw her agenda right away: She was calling about that older dog. Having pitched the retired donkeys many times before, she knew I wouldn't take them. And finding homes for adorable puppies is rarely a problem.

In fact, I made a few calls about the puppies, and placed two of them in minutes, giving the interested parties Amy's phone number. I didn't want to call her back myself; that was the safest course.

But the story of the older dog stuck in my head. I could envision a border collie behind a fence all day, probably wearing a groove in the dirt as he ran along the fence day and night.

I was a bit chewed up at the time, still dealing with the loss of my soulmate Orson. I'd had to put him down after he bit several people. His death was a recent wound and a big one, perhaps one that would never completely heal.

Yet the abandoned animal has always particularly touched me, even more than an abused one, oddly. Carol the Lonely Donkey was an example. Even Pearl, though hardly abused or neglected, had been in a crate at the veterinary clinic for many weeks while she recovered from surgery, a distressing isolation for so sociable a dog. I was eager to take her in, and she was happy to come.

A bit curious, and a bit apprehensive, I called Amy's friend Flo, who knew these dogs. She and Amy had teamed up to get the border collies into good homes before the farm was sold. It was a nice thing to do.

The older dog's name was Izzy, Flo said. He was a New Zealand–bred black-and-white, and he was "gorgeous."

He had spent several years in a small house built for dogs. It had no heat, so on particularly bitter nights, the caretaker took him into his trailer, but not often, since Izzy had never been housebroken. Otherwise, he lived in his little compound with an older, spayed female.

He and the caretaker's dog, a female border collie, did, in fact, run along the fences, the female on the outside, Izzy on the inside, wearing a deep trail. Then a few months ago, Izzy somehow escaped the fence, which was why there were now puppies.

"He's such a beautiful dog, but he's never been with people," said Flo, a friend of the caretaker. "Hard to place, because he's kind of wild, not trained, and not neutered. But he's a loving dog," she added quickly. "Very alert. Very tuned in to people when he sees them."

The farm owners, one a writer from the city, had bought the place a few years earlier and undertaken extensive renovations. They bought the border collies with the idea that they'd also acquire sheep. But they hadn't; in fact, they seemed to have given up on the idea of the farm altogether and hardly even showed up there.

Izzy was tended to by the caretaker. "He filled the food bowl," Flo reported, "and made sure the dogs had water. He didn't have time for much else."

I drove the half hour to the farm the next morning. It was a beautiful spread, with a carefully restored old farmhouse, a barn-turned-writer's-studio that I coveted, and acres of hills and meadows, gardens and ponds.

On the hill near where Flo and I had parked, I saw a black-and-white dog racing along the fence line, opposite a brown-and-white border collie running along outside.

"Izzy!" yelled Flo, but he barely responded. It occurred to me he might not know his name.

As we got closer, I could see that Flo was right: With his golden eyes and elegant—though badly matted—coat, he was a remarkably handsome dog, full of instinct and personality. He also seemed, like many working dogs that chase in circles all day, a bit mad.

Orson had been the same way when he came to me, which gave me pause. I loved Orson dearly, and he had done much for me, but his life had ended sorrowfully and too soon. I didn't want to experience anything like that again. Still, I had learned so much. Maybe I could get it right this time. That thought had drawn me since I'd first heard Amy's message.

Flo and I opened the gate and entered the compound. The older female scurried nervously into the dog house; a woman in Vermont had already agreed to take her in. Izzy raced over, ignored me, and jumped up on Flo. He was almost frantic, his tongue long on this warm Saturday.

He retreated long enough to give me a quick sniff and a bark, then rushed back to jump at Flo again, then dashed back along the fence. He dropped to the ground, spun around, so overjoyed to have some attention that he was hardly in control of himself.

I called him to me and offered him a treat; he didn't even notice it. But he lay down and showed me his belly, and I crouched down for a better look. His teeth seemed fine; his weight was perfect, his muscles firm. Except for the dirty, matted fur, he was in great condition, and eager for affection. But he'd need months, perhaps years, of training to calm down, and more appropriate work than running fences.

I wasn't sure he was for me. In such a state, he was too crazed to be a Bedlam Farm dog; he would drive me nuts. But I was sure that with a little training he'd be easy to place elsewhere.

I guess I'd kind of known this would happen.

ABOUT THE AUTHOR

JON KATZ has written sixteen books—six novels and ten works of nonfiction—including *Dog Days, A Dog Year, The Dogs of Bedlam Farm, The New Work of Dogs,* and *Katz on Dogs.* A two-time finalist for the National Magazine Award, he writes columns about dogs and rural life for the online magazine *Slate,* and has written for *The New York Times, The Wall Street Journal, Rolling Stone, GQ,* and the *AKC Gazette.* He cohosts an award-winning show, *Dog Talk,* on Northeast Public Radio. Katz lives on Bedlam Farm in upstate New York with his wife, Paula Span, and his dogs, sheep, steers and cow, donkeys, barn cat, irritable rooster Winston, and three hens. Visit www.bedlamfarm.com.

Discover Jon Katz and his lifetime of dogs

"This gentle book is a great reminder—as if anybody needed one—of what animals can mean to people at particular times in life."
—*The Atlanta Journal-Constitution*

"Moving, funny… a lovable mutt of a book."
—*Chicago Tribune*

"Katz's world—of animals and humans and their combined generosity of spirit—is a place you're glad you've been."
—*The Boston Globe*

"An inspiring portrait of the human-animal bond, *The Dogs of Bedlam Farm* traverses an emotional terrain that ranges from embattled spirit to celebratory energy. And it made me a Katz fan for life."
—*The Seattle Times*